FIX-IT and FORGET-IT®
Holiday Favorites

150 Easy and Delicious Slow Cooker Recipes

HOPE COMERFORD

Photos by Bonnie Matthews

Good Books

New York, New York

Visit our website at www.goodbooks.com.

10 9 8 7 6 5 4 3 2

Library of Congress Cataloging-in-Publication Data

Names: Comerford, Hope, author. | Matthews, Bonnie, 1963- photographer.
Title: Fix-it and forget-it holiday favorites: 150 easy and delicious slow
   cooker recipes / Hope Comerford ; photos by Bonnie Matthews.
Description: New York, New York: Good Books, [2017] | Includes index.
Identifiers: LCCN 2017014815| ISBN 9781680993301 (pbk.: alk. paper) | ISBN
   9781680993325 (Ebook)
Subjects: LCSH: Holiday cooking. | Electric cooking, Slow. | LCGFT: Cookbooks.
Classification: LCC TX739 .C572 2017 | DDC 641.5/884—dc23
LC record available at https://lccn.loc.gov/2017014815

Cover design by Jane Sheppard
Cover photo by Bonnie Matthews

Print ISBN: 978-1-68099-330-1
Ebook ISBN: 978-1-68099-332-5

Printed in the United States of America

Table of Contents

Welcome to Fix-It and Forget-It Holiday Favorites

The holidays are a very special time for our family. Like most families, the majority of our get-togethers revolve around food! Let's face it, we all love to eat (maybe my family more than most!). With a little help from our Fix-It and Forget-It friends from around the country, I've compiled 150 of the most popular Fix-It and Forget-It holiday recipes for you. You'll dazzle and wow your family, while the slow cooker helps you keep your sanity . . . and your food warm.

Whether you're hosting, celebrating with just a couple of friends, or bringing a dish to pass around for many at a large gathering, you'll find many forgiving and flexible recipes to choose from. There are recipes that only take a couple of hours to make, and there are recipes that cook for an extended period of time so you can tend to other important things.

The holidays can be a very stressful time, but cooking doesn't have to be. Put this book to good use and make it your own. Write little notes in the margins. Edit the ingredients to suit your personal tastes or needs. You'll find that planning a complete holiday menu has never been easier.

A Few Things You Should Know about Your Slow Cooker

Not all slow cookers are created equal . . . or work equally well for everyone!

Those of us who use slow cookers frequently know we have our own preferences when it comes to which slow cooker we choose to use. For instance, I love my programmable slow cooker, but there are many programmable slow cookers I've tried that I've strongly disliked. Why? Because some go by increments of 15 or 30 minutes and some go by 4, 6, 8, or 10 hours. I dislike those restrictions, but I have family and friends who don't mind them at all! I am also pretty brand loyal when it comes to my manual slow cookers because I've had great success with those and have had unsuccessful moments with slow cookers of other brands. So, which slow cooker(s) is/are best for your household?

It really depends on how many people you're feeding and if you're gone for long periods of time. Here are my recommendations:

For a 2–3-person household	3–5-quart slow cooker
For a 4–5-person household	5–6-quart slow cooker
For a ≥6- person household	6½–7-quart slow cooker

Large slow cooker advantages/disadvantages:

Advantages:
- You can fit a loaf pan or a baking dish into a 6- or 7-quart, depending on the shape of your cooker. That allows you to make bread or cakes, or even smaller quantities of main dishes. (Take your favorite baking dish and loaf pan along when you shop for a cooker to make sure they'll fit inside.)
- You can feed large groups of people, or make larger quantities of food, allowing for leftovers, or meals to freeze.

Disadvantages:
- They take up more storage room.
- They don't fit as neatly into a dishwasher.
- If your crock isn't ⅔–¾ full, you may burn your food.

Small slow cooker advantages/disadvantages:

Advantages:
- They're great for lots of appetizers, for serving hot drinks, for baking cakes straight in the crock, and for dorm rooms or apartments.
- They're a great option for making recipes of smaller quantities.

Disadvantages:
- Food in smaller quantities tends to cook more quickly than larger amounts. So keep an eye on it.
- Chances are, you won't have many leftovers. So, if you like to have leftovers, a smaller slow cooker may not be a good option for you.

My recommendation:

Have at least two slow cookers—one around 3–4 quarts and one 6 quarts or larger. A third would be a huge bonus (and a great advantage to your cooking repertoire!). The advantage of having at least a couple is that you can make a larger variety of recipes. Also, you can make at least two or three dishes at once for a whole meal.

Manual vs. Programmable

If you are gone for only 6–8 hours a day, a manual slow cooker might be just fine for you. If you are gone for more than 8 hours during the day, I would highly recommend purchasing a programmable slow cooker that will switch to warm when the cook time you set is up. It will allow you to cook a wider variety of recipes.

The two I use most frequently are my 4-quart manual slow cooker and my 6½-quart programmable slow cooker. I like that I can make smaller portions in my 4-quart slow cooker on days I don't need or want leftovers, but I also love how my 6½-quart slow cooker can accommodate whole chickens, turkey breasts, hams, or big batches of soups. I use them both often.

Get to Know Your Slow Cooker . . .

Plan a little time to get acquainted with your slow cooker. Each slow cooker has its own personality—just like your oven (and your car). Plus, many new slow cookers cook hotter and faster than earlier models. I think that with all of the concern for food safety, the slow cooker manufacturers have amped up their settings so that "High," "Low," and "Warm" are all higher temperatures than in the older models. That means they cook hotter—and therefore, faster—than the first slow cookers. The beauty of these little machines is that they're supposed to cook low and slow. We count on that when we flip the switch in the morning before we leave the house for 10 hours or so. So, because none of us knows what kind of temperament our slow cooker has until we try it out, nor how hot it cooks—don't assume anything. Save yourself a disappointment and make the first recipe in your new slow cooker on a day when you're at home. Cook it for the shortest amount of time the recipe calls for. Then, check the food to see if it's done. Or if you start smelling food that seems to be finished, turn off the cooker and rescue your food.

Also, all slow cookers seem to have a "hot spot," which is of great importance to know, especially when baking with your slow cooker. This spot may tend to burn food in that area if you're not careful. If you're baking directly in your slow cooker, I recommend covering the "hot spot" with some foil.

Tips and Tricks

Slow cookers tend to work best when they're ⅔–¾ of the way full. You may need to increase the cooking time if you've exceeded that amount, or reduce it if you've put in less than that. If you're going to exceed that limit, it would be best to reduce the recipe, or split it between two slow cookers. (Remember how I suggested owning at least two or three slow cookers?)

Keep your veggies on the bottom. That puts them in more direct contact with the heat. The fuller your slow cooker, the longer it will take its contents to cook. Also, the more densely packed the cooker's contents are, the longer they will take to cook. And finally, the larger the chunks of meat or vegetables, the more time they will need to cook.

Keep the lid on! Every time you take a peek, you lose 20 minutes of cooking time. Please take this into consideration each time you lift the lid! I know, some of you can't help yourself and are going to lift anyway. Just don't forget to tack on 20 minutes to your cook time for each time you peeked!

Sometimes it's beneficial to remove the lid. If you'd like your dish to thicken a bit, take the lid off during the last half hour to hour of cooking time.

If you have a big slow cooker (7–8-quart), you can cook a small batch in it by putting the recipe ingredients into an oven-safe baking dish or baking pan and then placing that into the cooker's crock. First, put a trivet or some metal jar rings on the bottom of the crock, and then set your dish or pan on top of them. Or a loaf pan may "hook onto" the top ridges of the crock belonging to a large oval cooker and hang there straight and securely, "baking" a cake or quick bread. Cover the cooker and flip it on.

The outside of your slow cooker will be hot! Please remember to keep it out of reach of children and keep that in mind for yourself as well!

Get yourself a quick-read meat thermometer and use it! This helps remove the question of whether or not your meat is fully cooked, and helps prevent you from overcooking your meat as well.

Internal cooking temperatures:
- Beef—125–130°F (rare); 140–145°F (medium); 160°F (well-done)
- Pork—140–145°F (rare); 145–150°F (medium); 160°F (well-done)
- Turkey and Chicken—165°F
- Frozen meat: The basic rule of thumb is, don't put frozen meat into the slow cooker. The meat does not reach the proper internal temperature in time. This especially applies to thick cuts of meat! Proceed with caution!

- Add fresh herbs 10 minutes before the end of the cooking time to maximize their flavor.
- If your recipe calls for cooked pasta, add it 10 minutes before the end of the cooking time if the cooker is on High; 30 minutes before the end of the cooking time if it's on Low. Then the pasta won't get mushy.
- If your recipe calls for sour cream or cream, stir it in 5 minutes before the end of the cooking time. You want it to heat but not boil or simmer.

Approximate slow cooker temperatures (remember, each slow cooker is different):
- High—212–300°F
- Low—170–200°F
- Simmer—185°F
- Warm—165°F

Cooked beans freeze well. Store them in freezer bags (squeeze the air out first) or freezer boxes. Cooked and dried bean measurements:
- 16-oz. can, drained = about 1¾ cups beans
- 19-oz. can, drained = about 2 cups beans
- 1 lb. dried beans (about 2½ cups) = 5 cups cooked beans

Appetizers, Snacks, and Spreads

Red Currant Meatballs

Hope Comerford, Clinton Township, MI

Makes 16–20 servings
Prep. Time: 5 minutes & Cooking Time: 6 hours & Ideal slow-cooker size: 5-qt.

2 12-oz. jars red currant jelly

12 oz. chili sauce

½ cup minced onions

16-oz. can pineapple bits, drained

48 oz. frozen meatballs

1. Mix together the jelly, chili sauce, and minced onions. Stir in the pineapple bits.

2. Spray the crock with nonstick spray, then add in the meatballs.

3. Pour the sauce over the meatballs and stir.

4. Cover and cook on Low for 6 hours.

Cranberry Meatballs

Char Hagner, Montague, MI

Makes about 50–60 meatballs
Prep. Time: 30–45 minutes ❧ Cooking Time: 2 hours ❧ Ideal slow-cooker size: 3–4-qt.

Meatballs:

2 lb. ground beef

⅓ cup parsley flakes

2 Tbsp. soy sauce

½ tsp. garlic powder

2 Tbsp. minced onions

1 cup cornflake crumbs

2 eggs

½ cup ketchup

Sauce:

1 can jellied cranberry sauce

12-oz. bottle chili sauce

2 Tbsp. brown sugar

1 Tbsp. lemon juice

1. In a large mixing bowl, combine meatball ingredients until well mixed.

2. Form into 50–60 meatballs and put in lightly greased 9x13-inch baking pan.

3. Bake at 350°F for about 30 minutes, or until meatballs are cooked through. (Cut one open to test.)

4. While meatballs are baking, combine sauce ingredients in saucepan. Heat over low heat until jellied sauce and brown sugar melt. Stir frequently.

5. Place baked meatballs in slow cooker. Pour sauce over meatballs, making sure that all are covered in sauce if you've layered them in the cooker.

6. Cover. Cook on Low 2 hours, or until sauce is bubbly.

7. Turn slow cooker to Warm and serve with toothpicks.

Variations:

1. Use 1 lb. ground beef and 1 lb. ground pork instead of 2 lb. ground beef.

2. Use 10¾-oz. can condensed tomato soup, mixed with 1 tsp. prepared mustard, instead of chili sauce. —Jane Geigley, Honey Brook, PA

3. Here's an alternative meatball recipe:

2 egg whites
2 lb. ground turkey
2 green onions with tops, sliced
4 tsp. grated orange peel

2 tsp. reduced-sodium soy sauce
½ tsp. black pepper
⅛ tsp. cayenne pepper, *optional*

Use alternative meatball ingredients for Steps 1–3 above, and then continue with rest of recipe.
—Mary Ann Bowman, East Earl, PA

Ham Balls

Jo Haberkamp, Fairbank, IA

Makes 12–16 servings
Prep. Time: 30 minutes & Cooking Time: 4–5 hours & Ideal slow-cooker size: 6-qt.

Ham Balls:

3 eggs

3 cups crushed graham crackers

2 cups milk

1 tsp. salt

1 tsp. onion salt

¼ tsp. pepper

2 lb. ground ham

1½ lb. ground beef

1½ lb. ground pork

Topping:

½ cup ketchup

¼ cup water

1 cup brown sugar

¼ cup plus 2 Tbsp. apple cider vinegar

½ tsp. dry mustard

1. Beat eggs slightly in large bowl. Add graham crackers, milk, salt, onion salt, pepper, and ground meats. Mix well.

2. Form into 24 balls, using ½-cup measuring cup for each ball.

3. In a separate bowl, combine topping ingredients.

4. Layer ham balls and topping in greased slow cooker. Make sure each layer of ham balls is well-covered with topping.

5. Cover. Cook on High 1 hour. Reduce heat to Low and cook 3–4 hours more, or until meat is cooked through but not dried out.

Cranberry Franks

Loretta Krahn, Mountain Lake, MN

Makes 15–20 servings
Prep. Time: 10 minutes ⚜ *Cooking Time: 1–2 hours* ⚜ *Ideal slow-cooker size: 3-qt.*

2 pkgs. cocktail wieners, or little smoked sausages

16-oz. can jellied cranberry sauce

1 cup ketchup

3 Tbsp. brown sugar

1 Tbsp. lemon juice

1. Combine all ingredients in slow cooker.

2. Cover. Cook on High 1–2 hours.

NOTE
Great picnic, potluck, or buffet food.

Sweet and Sour Chicken Wings

H. Schoen, Windsor, CT

Makes 6–8 servings

Prep. Time: 15 minutes 🔥 Cooking Time: 7 hours 🔥 Ideal slow-cooker size: 3–4-qt.

1½ cups sugar

1 cup cider vinegar

½ cup ketchup

1 chicken bouillon cube

2 Tbsp. soy sauce

¼ tsp. salt, *optional*

¼ tsp. pepper, *optional*

16 chicken wings

¼ cup cornstarch

½ cup cold water

1. On stove in medium-sized saucepan, mix together sugar, vinegar, ketchup, bouillon cube, soy sauce, and salt and pepper if you wish.

2. Bring to a boil over medium heat. Stir to dissolve sugar and bouillon cube.

3. Put wings in slow cooker. Pour sauce over wings.

4. Cover. Simmer on Low 6½ hours, or until wings are tender but not dry.

5. A few minutes before end of cooking time, combine cornstarch and water in a small bowl. When smooth, stir gently into wings and sauce.

6. Cover. Simmer on High until liquid thickens, about 30 minutes.

7. To serve, keep cooker turned to Low. Stir occasionally.

Sweet Chili Chicken Bites

Nanci Keatley, Salem, OR

Makes 4 cups

Prep. Time: 10 minutes ❧ Cooking Time: 4–6 hours ❧ Ideal slow-cooker size: 4-qt.

4 lb. boneless skinless chicken breasts

1 bottle Asian sweet chili sauce
(we use Mae Ploy brand)

1. Cut chicken into bite-sized pieces. Place in slow cooker.

2. Pour bottle of sauce over chicken. Stir together well.

3. Cover. Cook on Low 4–6 hours, or until chicken is fully cooked.

4. Serve with toothpicks.

TIP
from Tester
This is also good as
a main dish served
over cooked rice.

Creamy Artichoke Dip

Jessica Stoner, West Liberty, OH

Makes 7–8 cups
Prep. Time: 15–20 minutes & Cooking Time: 1–1½ hours & Ideal slow-cooker size: 3-qt.

2 14-oz. cans water-packed artichoke hearts, coarsely chopped (drain one can; stir juice from other can into dip)

2 cups (8 oz.) shredded, part-skim mozzarella cheese

8-oz. pkg. cream cheese, softened

1 cup grated Parmesan cheese

½ cup shredded Swiss cheese

½ cup mayonnaise

2 Tbsp. lemon juice

2 Tbsp. plain yogurt

1 Tbsp. seasoned salt

1 Tbsp. chopped, seeded jalapeño pepper

1 tsp. garlic powder

tortilla chips

1. In slow cooker, combine artichoke hearts and juice from one can, cheeses, mayonnaise, lemon juice, yogurt, seasoned salt, jalapeño pepper, and garlic powder.

2. Cover. Cook on Low 1 hour, or until cheeses are melted and dip is heated through.

3. Serve with tortilla chips.

Variation:

Add 2 10-oz. pkgs. frozen chopped spinach, thawed and squeezed dry, to Step 1. —Steven Lantz, Denver, CO

Red Pepper Cheese Dip

Ann Bender, Fort Defiance, VA

Makes 4–5 cups
Prep. Time: 10 minutes ⚜ *Cooking Time: 2 hours* ⚜ *Ideal slow-cooker size: 3-qt.*

2 Tbsp. olive oil

4–6 large red peppers, cut into 1-inch squares

crackers and/or pita bread

½ lb. feta cheese, crumbled

1. Pour oil into slow cooker. Stir in peppers.

2. Cover. Cook on Low 2 hours.

3. Serve on crackers or pita bread, topped with feta cheese.

Serving Suggestion:
Drizzle plate with balsamic vinegar.

Bacon Cheese Dip

Genelle Taylor, Perrysburg, OH

Makes 6 cups

Prep. Time: 10–20 minutes ❧ *Cooking Time: 2 hours or less* ❧ *Ideal slow-cooker size: 3-qt.*

2 8-oz. pkgs. cream cheese, cubed

4 cups shredded sharp cheddar cheese

1 cup half-and-half

2 tsp. Worcestershire sauce

1 tsp. minced dried onion

1 tsp. prepared mustard

16 bacon strips, cooked and crumbled

tortilla chips and/or French bread slices

1. Combine first six ingredients in slow cooker.

2. Cover. Cook on Low 2 hours, or until cheeses are melted. Stir occasionally if you're home and able to do so.

3. Just before serving, stir in bacon.

4. Serve warm with tortilla chips and/or sliced French bread.

Creamy Pizza Dip

Rosalie Buckwalter, Narvon, PA

Makes 4½ cups
Prep. Time: 15–20 minutes ⚭ Cooking Time: 2–4 hours ⚭ Ideal slow-cooker size: 3-qt.

8-oz. pkg. cream cheese, cubed and softened

¾ cup salad dressing, or mayonnaise (regular or light)

1 cup shredded mozzarella cheese

8 oz. sliced pepperoni, chopped

2 ripe plum tomatoes, chopped

10 large, black olives, chopped

4 crusty Italian rolls, toasted if you wish, and then cut into ½-inch cubes, and/or crackers

1. Mix all ingredients, except rolls and crackers for dipping, in slow cooker.

2. Cover. Cook on High 2–4 hours, or until cheese is melted and dip is heated through.

3. Turn on Low to keep warm while serving.

4. Remove cover. Allow to cool slightly before serving with rolls and/or crackers for dipping.

Nacho Dip

Rose Hankins, Stevensville, MD

Makes 3–4 cups
Prep. Time: 5 minutes ☙ Cooking Time: 3–4 hours ☙ Ideal slow-cooker size: 4 qt.

4 cups (16 oz.) shredded cheddar cheese

14-oz. can diced tomatoes, drained, with juice reserved

7-oz. can chopped green chilies, drained

1 cup chopped onions

1 Tbsp. cumin

1 tsp. chili powder

1 tsp. hot pepper sauce

tortilla chips

1. Mix cheese, drained tomatoes, drained chilies, onions, cumin, chili powder, and hot pepper sauce in slow cooker.

2. Cover. Cook on Low 3–4 hours.

3. Stir before serving. If dip is stiffer than you like, stir in some of the reserved tomato juice.

4. Serve with tortilla chips for dipping.

Cheesy Hot Bean Dip

John D. Allen, Rye, CO

Makes 4–5 cups

Prep. Time: 10 minutes   ♣   Cooking Time: 2 hours   ♣   Ideal slow-cooker size: 2-qt.

16-oz. can refried beans

1 cup salsa

2 cups (8 oz.) shredded Monterey Jack
and cheddar cheeses, mixed

1 cup sour cream

3-oz. pkg. cream cheese, cubed

1 Tbsp. chili powder

¼ tsp. ground cumin

tortilla chips

1. Combine all ingredients except tortilla chips in slow cooker.

2. Cover. Cook on High 2 hours. Stir 2–3 times during cooking time.

3. Serve warm from cooker with tortilla chips.

NOTE

This bean dip is a favorite of ours. Once you start on it, it's hard to leave it alone. We have been known to dip into it even when it's cold.

Serving Suggestion:
Drizzle with hot sauce and top with diced avocado.

Cheese and Crab Dip

Donna Lantgen, Rapid City, SD

Makes 5 cups
Prep. Time: 10 minutes ❧ Cooking Time: 2 hours ❧ Ideal slow-cooker size: 2-qt.

3 8-oz. pkgs. cream cheese, softened
2 6-oz. cans crabmeat, drained
1 4-oz. can tiny shrimp, drained
6 Tbsp. finely chopped onions
1 tsp. horseradish
½ cup toasted almonds
assorted crackers and/or bread cubes

1. Combine all ingredients, except toasted almonds, crackers and/or bread cubes, in slow cooker.

2. Cover. Cook on Low 2 hours.

3. Sprinkle with toasted almonds. Serve with crackers or bread cubes.

Serving Suggestion:
Dust with paprika.

Variation:
Add 2 tsp. Worcestershire sauce to Step 1 for added zest. —Dorothy VanDeest, Memphis, TN

Spicy Party Mix

Sharon Miller, Holmesville, OH

Makes 13 cups

Prep. Time: 15 minutes ⚬ *Cooking Time: 3–4 hours* ⚬ *Ideal slow-cooker size: 4–5-qt.*

¾ stick (6 Tbsp.) butter, melted

1-oz. packet taco seasoning mix

¾ tsp. ground cinnamon

⅛–¼ tsp. cayenne, depending on your taste preference

2 cups pecan halves

2 cups roasted cashews, unsalted

2 cups walnut halves

2 cups whole almonds, unblanched

3 cups Goldfish, or bite-sized cheese crackers

2 cups pretzel nuggets or sticks

1. Mix butter and seasonings in slow cooker.

2. Add all remaining ingredients and toss together gently.

3. Cook uncovered on Low 3–4 hours, stirring every 30 minutes until nuts are toasted. Turn off heat.

4. Serve from slow cooker with large spoon, or pour into big serving bowl.

TIP

You can make this a day before your party. Just be sure to store it in an airtight container.

Christmas Sugared Walnuts

Lavina Hochstedler, Grand Blanc, MI

Makes 3–4 cups

Prep. Time: 10 minutes ⚜ *Cooking Time: 2–3 hours* ⚜ *Ideal slow-cooker size: 2–3-qt.*

1 lb. walnut pieces
1 stick (8 Tbsp.) unsalted butter, melted
½ cup confectioners' sugar
1½ tsp. ground cinnamon
¼ tsp. ground ginger
¼ tsp. ground allspice
⅛ tsp. ground cloves

1. In slow cooker, stir walnuts and butter together until combined.

2. Add confectioners' sugar, stirring to coat nuts evenly.

3. Cover. Cook on High 15 minutes. Then reduce heat to Low.

4. Cook uncovered, stirring occasionally, until nuts are coated with a crisp glaze, about 2 hours.

5. Transfer nuts to a serving bowl.

6. In a small bowl, combine spices. Sift over nuts, stirring to coat evenly.

7. Cool nuts completely before serving.

Caramel Peanut Butter Dip

Genelle Taylor, Perrysburg, OH

Makes about 1½ cups
Prep. Time: 20 minutes & *Ideal slow-cooker size: 1-qt.*

30 caramels, unwrapped

1–2 Tbsp. water

¼ cup plus 2 Tbsp. creamy peanut butter

¼ cup finely crushed peanuts, *optional*

sliced apples, unpeeled

1. In a microwave-safe bowl, microwave caramels and water for 1 minute on High. Stir. Microwave 1 minute more, or until smooth.

2. Add peanut butter and mix well. Microwave 30 seconds on High, or until smooth.

3. Stir in peanuts if you wish.

4. Transfer to a 1-qt. slow cooker. Turn to Warm while serving.

5. Serve with sliced apples.

NOTE
Red and green apples look very festive for the holiday season.

Chunky Spiced Apple Butter

Jennifer Freed, Harrisonburg, VA

Makes 4 cups

Prep. Time: 20 minutes & Cooking Time: 8 hours & Ideal slow-cooker size: 2–3-qt.

4 cups (about 1 ¼ lb.) peeled, chopped Granny Smith apples

¾ cup packed dark brown sugar

2 Tbsp. balsamic vinegar

½ stick (4 Tbsp.) butter, *divided*

1 Tbsp. ground cinnamon

½ tsp. salt

¼ tsp. ground cloves

1 ½ tsp. vanilla extract

1. Combine apples, sugar, vinegar, 2 Tbsp. butter, cinnamon, salt, and cloves in slow cooker.

2. Cover. Cook on Low 8 hours.

3. Stir in remaining 2 Tbsp. butter and vanilla.

4. Cool completely before serving, storing, or giving away.

Pumpkin Butter

Emily Fox, Bethel, PA

Makes approximately 6½ cups
Prep. Time: 5–10 minutes ♣ Cooking Time: 11–12 hours ♣ Ideal slow-cooker size: 3-qt.

6 cups pumpkin puree

2¾ cups light brown sugar

2½ tsp. pumpkin pie spice

1. Mix pumpkin puree, brown sugar, and pumpkin pie spice together in slow cooker.

2. Cook uncovered on Low for 11–12 hours, depending on how thick you'd like the butter to be. Cool.

3. Serve on bread or rolls for seasonal eating.

NOTE
Refrigerate or freeze until ready to use.

TIP
from Tester

You could replace 3 cups pumpkin puree with 3 cups applesauce for a different twist on pumpkin butter.

Pear Butter

Betty Moore, Plano, IL

Makes 2–3 pts.
Prep. Time: 15 minutes ❧ Cooking Time: 11–13 hours ❧ Ideal slow-cooker size: 4-qt.

10 large pears (about 4 lb.)
1 cup orange juice
2½ cups sugar
1 tsp. ground cinnamon
1 tsp. ground cloves
½ tsp. ground allspice

1. Peel and quarter pears. Place in slow cooker.

2. Cover. Cook on Low 10–12 hours. Drain. Discard liquid.

3. Mash or puree pears. Add remaining ingredients. Mix well and return to slow cooker.

4. Cover. Cook on High 1 hour.

5. Place in hot sterile jars and process, following the instructions of your canning equipment. Allow to cool undisturbed for 24 hours.

Breakfast and Brunch Dishes

Turkey Bacon, Spinach, and Gruyère Quiche

Hope Comerford, Clinton Township, MI

Makes 4–6 servings
Prep. Time: 15 minutes   ❧   *Cooking Time: 3–4 hours*   ❧   *Ideal slow-cooker size: 6-qt.*

8 eggs

I cup milk

I tsp. salt

I tsp. pepper

I tsp. garlic powder

I tsp. onion powder

½ cup chopped onions

5 slices turkey bacon, diced

2 handfuls (about 2 oz.) fresh spinach leaves

8 oz. Gruyère cheese, shredded

1. In a bowl, mix together the eggs, milk, salt, pepper, garlic powder, and onion powder. Pour this into the bottom of your greased crock.

2. Sprinkle the onions and bacon evenly over the surface of the eggs.

3. Spread the spinach all over the top of the egg mixture in your crock.

4. Cover the spinach with the shredded cheese.

5. Cover and cook on Low for 3–4 hours, or until it is completely set in the middle.

Western Omelet Casserole

Mary Louise Martin, Boyd, WI
Jan Mast, Lancaster, PA

Makes 10 servings

Prep. Time: 15 minutes ❧ Cooking Time: 4–6 hours ❧ Ideal slow-cooker size: 5-qt.

32-oz. bag frozen hash brown potatoes, *divided*

1 lb. cooked ham, cubed, *divided*

1 medium onion, diced, *divided*

1½ cups shredded cheddar cheese, *divided*

18 eggs

1½ cups milk

1 tsp. salt

1 tsp. pepper

1. Layer ⅓ each of frozen potatoes, ham, onion, and cheese in bottom of slow cooker. Repeat 2 times.

2. Beat together eggs, milk, salt, and pepper in a large mixing bowl. Pour over mixture in slow cooker.

3. Cover. Cook on Low 4–6 hours.

Serving Suggestion:
Top with diced tomatoes or diced red peppers.

NOTE
This is a great breakfast, served along with orange juice and fresh fruit.

Eggs 'n Spinach

Shirley Unternahrer, Wayland, IA

Makes 8 servings
Prep. Time: 20 minutes & Cooking Time: 1½–8 hours & Ideal slow-cooker size: 6-qt.

1 lb. sausage with bacon (Farmland offers Original Pork & Bacon Link Sausage)

15-oz. frozen spinach, thawed and squeezed dry

⅓ cup plus 2 Tbsp. grated Parmesan cheese, *divided*

8 eggs

⅛ tsp. black pepper, ground or cracked

1. Sauté sausage in skillet until browned. Drain off half the drippings.

2. Coat interior of slow cooker with cooking spray. Place sausage and reserved drippings in slow cooker.

3. Stir spinach into slow cooker.

4. Stir in ⅓ cup Parmesan cheese.

5. Crack eggs directly onto mixture in slow cooker. Be careful not to break yolks. Do not stir.

6. Cover. Cook on High 1½ hours, or on Low up to 8 hours (you can turn it on right before you go to bed).

7. Sprinkle with pepper and 2 Tbsp. Parmesan cheese before serving.

Breakfast Skillet

Sue Hamilton, Minooka, IL

Makes 4–5 servings
Prep. Time: 15 minutes & Cooking Time: 2½–6 hours & Ideal slow-cooker size: 3½-qt.

3 cups milk
5½-oz. box au gratin potatoes
1 tsp. hot sauce
5 eggs, lightly beaten
1 Tbsp. prepared mustard
4-oz. can sliced mushrooms, drained
8 slices bacon, fried and crumbled
1 cup shredded cheddar cheese

1. Combine milk, au gratin sauce packet, hot sauce, eggs, and mustard in slow cooker until well blended.

2. Stir in dried potatoes, drained mushrooms, and bacon.

3. Cover. Cook on High 2½–3 hours, or on Low 5–6 hours.

4. Sprinkle cheese over top. Cover and let stand a few minutes until cheese melts.

Slow-Cooker Oatmeal

Betty B. Dennison, Grove City, PA

Makes 2 servings
Prep. Time: 5 minutes   ♣   Cooking Time: 6–8 hours   ♣   Ideal slow-cooker size: 1½-qt.

1 cup uncooked rolled oats
2 cups water
salt
⅓–½ cup raisins
¼ tsp. ground nutmeg
¼ tsp. ground cinnamon

1. Combine all ingredients in slow cooker.

2. Cover. Cook on Low 6–8 hours.

3. Eat warm with milk and brown sugar.

Apple Oatmeal

Sheila Plock, Boalsburg, PA

Makes 6–8 servings
Prep. Time: 15 minutes & Cooking Time: 6 hours & Ideal slow-cooker size: 5-qt.

3–4 apples, peeled and sliced
½ cup brown sugar
1 tsp. nutmeg
1 tsp. cinnamon
¼ stick (2 Tbsp.) butter, cut in chunks
½ cup walnuts
3 cups uncooked rolled oats
6 cups milk

1. Layer apples in bottom of slow cooker.

2. Sprinkle with brown sugar, nutmeg, and cinnamon.

3. Dot with butter.

4. Scatter walnuts evenly over top.

5. Layer oats over fruit and nuts.

6. Pour milk over oats. Stir together until well blended.

7. Cover. Cook on Low 6 hours.

NOTE
Wake up to the smell of freshly baked apple pie!

Oatmeal Morning

Barbara Forrester Landis, Lititz, PA

Makes 6 servings
Prep. Time: 5 minutes ꙮ Cooking Time: 2½–6 hours ꙮ Ideal slow-cooker size: 3-qt.

1 cup uncooked steel cut oats

1 cup dried cranberries

1 cup walnuts

½ tsp. salt

1 Tbsp. cinnamon

4 cups liquid (milk, water, or combination of the two)

1. Combine all dry ingredients in slow cooker. Stir well.

2. Pour in milk and/or water. Mix together well.

3. Cover. Cook on High 2½ hours or on Low 5–6 hours.

Variation:

If you wish, substitute fresh or dried blueberries, or raisins, for the dried cranberries.

Fruits and Grains Breakfast Cereal

Jean M. Butzer, Batavia, NY
Katrina Eberly, Wernersville, PA

Makes 10 servings
Prep. Time: 10 minutes   Cooking Time: 6–7 hours   Ideal slow-cooker size: 5-qt.

5 cups water

2 cups uncooked whole-grain cereal of your choice

1 medium apple, peeled and chopped

1 cup unsweetened apple juice

¼ cup chopped dried apricots

¼ cup dried cranberries

¼ cup raisins

¼ cup chopped dates

2–4 Tbsp. maple syrup, according to your preference for sweetness

1 tsp. cinnamon

½ tsp. salt

1. Combine all ingredients in slow cooker.

2. Cover. Cook on Low 6–7 hours, or until fruits and grains are as soft as you like them.

NOTE

This hearty breakfast dish reminds me of the old-fashioned oatmeal that was a winter staple in our country kitchen many years ago. My dad would put it on to cook before he went to the barn to milk cows. It would be cooked to perfection by the time he was done with chores and ready for breakfast.
—Jean M. Butzer, Batavia, NY

Hot Wheat Berry Cereal

Rosemarie Fitzgerald, Gibsonia, PA

Makes 4 servings

Prep. Time: 5 minutes ❧ *Soaking Time: 8 hours* ❧ *Cooking Time: 10 hours* ❧ *Ideal slow-cooker size: 3-qt.*

I cup dry wheat berries

5 cups water

honey

milk

butter

1. Rinse and sort wheat berries. Cover with water and soak 8 hours in slow cooker.

2. Cover. Cook on Low overnight (or up to 10 hours).

3. Drain, if needed. Serve hot with honey, milk, and butter.

NOTE

Wheat berries can also be used in pilafs or grain salads. Cook as indicated, drain, and cool. If you have trouble finding wheat berries, you can substitute farro.

Variation:

Eat your hot wheat berries with raisins and maple syrup as a variation.

Mexican-Style Grits

Mary Sommerfeld, Lancaster, PA

Makes 10–12 servings
Prep. Time: 10 minutes   ⚬   Cooking Time: 2 6 hours   ⚬   Ideal slow-cooker size: 3-qt.

1½ cups instant grits
1 lb. Velveeta cheese, cubed
½ tsp. garlic powder
2 4-oz. cans diced chilies, drained
1 stick (8 Tbsp.) butter, cut in chunks

1. Prepare grits according to package directions.

2. Stir in cheese, garlic powder, and chilies, until cheese is melted.

3. Stir in butter. Pour into greased slow cooker.

4. Cover. Cook on High 2–3 hours, or on Low 4–6 hours.

Serving Suggestion:
Top with paprika or cayenne pepper.

Cornmeal Mush

Betty Hostetler, Allensville, PA

Makes 15–18 servings
Prep. Time: 5–10 minutes & Cooking Time: 4–6 hours & Ideal slow-cooker size: 4-qt.

2 cups cornmeal
2 tsp. salt
2 cups cold water
6 cups hot water

1. Combine cornmeal, salt, and cold water in greased slow cooker.

2. Pour in hot water, stirring until well blended.

3. Cover. Cook on High 1 hour. Stir well. Cook on Low 3–4 hours. (Or cook on Low 5–6 hours, stirring once every hour during the first 2 hours.)

Serving Suggestion:
Serve hot with butter alongside for those who want to add a chunk to their individual servings. Or serve warm with milk and syrup.

Variation:

Pour cooked cornmeal mush into loaf pans. Chill until set (several hours or overnight). Cut into ½-inch-thick slices. Dredge each slice in flour. Melt a tablespoon of butter in large skillet. Fry slices in butter, being careful not to crowd the skillet or mush will steam and not brown. When the first side is well browned, flip each slice to brown the other side.

Breakfast Apple Cobbler

Anona M. Teel, Bangor, PA

Makes 6–8 servings
Prep. Time: 15 minutes ❧ Cooking Time: 2–9 hours ❧ Ideal slow-cooker size: 3½–4-qt.

8 medium apples, peeled, cored, and sliced

¼ cup sugar

dash of cinnamon

juice of 1 lemon

½ stick (4 Tbsp.) butter, melted

2 cups granola

1. Combine all ingredients in slow cooker.

2. Cover. Cook on Low 7–9 hours (while you sleep), or on High 2–3 hours (after you're up in the morning).

Hot Apple Breakfast

Colleen Konetzni, Rio Rancho, NM

Makes 8 servings
Prep. Time: 15 minutes   ⚓   Cooking Time: 8–10 hours   ⚓   Ideal slow-cooker size: 3½-qt.

10 apples, peeled and sliced

½–1 cup sugar, according to the sweetness of the apples and your taste preference

1 Tbsp. ground cinnamon

¼ tsp. ground nutmeg

1. Combine all ingredients in slow cooker.
2. Cover. Cook on Low 8–10 hours.

Serving Suggestion:

This is yummy over oatmeal or mixed with vanilla yogurt. Or serve it over pancakes or waffles.

Variation:

Add chopped nuts for an extra treat, either before cooking or before serving.

Breakfast Prunes

Jo Haberkamp, Fairbank, IA

Makes 6 servings
Prep. Time: 10 minutes ❧ Cooking Time: 8–10 hours ❧ Ideal slow-cooker size: 2-qt.

2 cups orange juice
¼ cup orange marmalade
1 tsp. ground cinnamon
¼ tsp. ground cloves
¼ tsp. ground nutmeg
1 cup water
12-oz. pkg. pitted dried prunes (1¾ cups)
2 thin lemon slices

1. Combine orange juice, marmalade, cinnamon, cloves, nutmeg, and water in slow cooker.

2. Stir in prunes and lemon slices.

3. Cover. Cook on Low 8–10 hours, or overnight.

4. Serve warm as a breakfast food, or warm or chilled as a side dish with a meal later in the day.

Variation:

If you prefer more citrus flavor, eliminate the ground cloves and reduce the cinnamon to ½ tsp. and the nutmeg to ⅛ tsp.

Boston Brown Bread

Jean M. Butzer, Batavia, NY

Makes 3 loaves

Prep. Time: 15–20 minutes ⚶ *Cooking Time: 4 hours* ⚶ *Ideal slow-cooker size: large enough to hold 3 cans upright*

3 16-oz. vegetable cans, cleaned and emptied

½ cup rye flour

½ cup yellow cornmeal

½ cup whole wheat flour

3 Tbsp. sugar

1 tsp. baking soda

¾ tsp. salt

½ cup chopped walnuts

½ cup raisins

1 cup buttermilk

⅓ cup molasses

TIP

To substitute for buttermilk, pour 1 Tbsp. lemon juice into a 1-cup measure. Add enough milk to fill the cup. Let stand 5 minutes before mixing with molasses.

1. Spray insides of cans, and one side of 3 6-inch-square pieces of foil, with nonstick cooking spray. Set aside.

2. Combine rye flour, cornmeal, whole wheat flour, sugar, baking soda, and salt in a large bowl.

3. Stir in walnuts and raisins.

4. Whisk together buttermilk and molasses in a separate bowl. Add to dry ingredients. Stir until well mixed. Spoon into prepared cans.

5. Place one piece of foil, greased side down, on top of each can. Secure foil with rubber bands or cotton string. Place upright in slow cooker.

6. Pour boiling water into slow cooker to come halfway up sides of cans. (Make sure foil tops do not touch boiling water.)

7. Cover cooker. Cook on Low 4 hours, or until skewer inserted in center of bread comes out clean.

8. To remove bread, lay cans on their sides. Roll and tap gently on all sides until bread releases. Cool completely on wire racks.

9. Serve with butter or cream cheese.

Soups, Stews, and Chilis

Creamy Butternut Squash Soup

Hope Comerford, Clinton Township, MI

Makes 4–6 servings
Prep. Time: 20 minutes & Cooking Time: 8 hours & Ideal slow-cooker size: 3-qt.

1½ lb. butternut squash, peeled and cut into 1-inch chunks

1 small onion, quartered

1 carrot, cut into 1-inch chunks

1 small sweet potato, cut into 1-inch chunks

¼ tsp. cinnamon

⅛ tsp. nutmeg

½ tsp. sugar

¼ tsp salt

⅛ tsp. pepper

⅛ tsp. ginger

3 cups chicken stock (or you can use vegetable stock to keep this vegetarian)

1 cup heavy cream or half-and-half

1. Place the butternut squash, onion, carrot, and sweet potato pieces into your crock.

2. Sprinkle the contents of the crock with the cinnamon, nutmeg, sugar, salt, pepper, and ginger. Pour the stock over the top.

3. Cover and cook on Low for 8 hours, or until the vegetables are soft.

4. Using an immersion blender, blend the soup until smooth.

5. Remove ¼ cup of the soup and mix it with 1 cup of heavy cream or half-and-half. Pour this into the crock and mix until well combined.

Butternut Squash and Apple Soup

Tina Hartman, Lancaster, PA

Makes 25–28 1-cup servings

Prep. Time: 30–60 minutes ⚬ *Cooking Time: 1–2 hours* ⚬ *Ideal slow-cooker size: 8–qt.*

¼ stick (2 Tbsp.) unsalted butter

2 Tbsp. olive oil

4 cups chopped yellow onions

2 Tbsp. mild curry powder

5 lb. butternut squash (2 large ones)

1½ lb. sweet apples

2 tsp. salt

½ tsp. ground pepper

2 cups water

2 cups apple cider, or juice

1. Warm butter, olive oil, onions, and curry powder in large stockpot over low heat on stove until onions are tender (15 to 20 minutes).

2. Peel squash and remove seeds. Cut squash into chunks.

3. Peel, core, and cut apples into about 8 wedges each.

4. Add squash, apples, salt, pepper, and water to butter mixture in stockpot. Cook until soft enough to puree.

5. Puree or process with a food processor.

6. Pour entire mixture into slow cooker. Add apple cider or juice.

7. Cover. Cook on Low 1–2 hours. Serve hot from the cooker.

NOTE

This recipe is actually from my friends Brittany Leffler and Brian McKee. (They should get credit for it!) They host a cookie-exchange party every Christmas, and they serve this and chili. The rest of us bring the cookies. It is wonderful.

Cream of Pumpkin Soup

Nanci Keatley, Salem, OR

Makes 4–6 servings

Prep. Time: 10–15 minutes 🌿 Cooking Time: 3–4 hours 🌿 Ideal slow-cooker size: 4-qt.

1 Tbsp. butter, melted
1 large onion, diced fine
32-oz. vegetable stock
16-oz. can solid-pack pumpkin
1 tsp. salt
¼ tsp. cinnamon
¼ tsp. freshly ground nutmeg
⅛ tsp. ground ginger
⅛ tsp. ground cloves
⅛ tsp. ground cardamom
¼ tsp. freshly ground pepper
1 ½ cups half-and-half
1 cup heavy cream
chopped chives

1. Mix butter and onion in slow cooker.

2. Add stock, pumpkin, salt, and other seasonings. Mix well.

3. Cover. Cook on Low 2–3 hours.

4. Add half-and-half and cream.

5. Cover. Cook on Low 1 hour, or until heated through.

6. Garnish individual serving bowls with chives.

Creamy Tomato Soup

Susie Shenk Wenger, Lancaster, PA

Makes 4 servings
Prep. Time: 10–15 minutes & Cooking Time: 3–4 hours & Ideal slow-cooker size: 3-qt.

29-oz. can tomato sauce, or crushed tomatoes, or 1 qt. home-canned tomatoes, chopped

1 small onion, chopped

1–2 carrots, sliced thin

2 tsp. brown sugar

1 tsp. Italian seasoning

¼ tsp. salt

¼ tsp. pepper

1 tsp. freshly chopped parsley

½ tsp. Worcestershire sauce

1 cup heaving whipping cream

croutons, preferably homemade

freshly grated Parmesan cheese

1. Combine tomato sauce, onion, carrots, brown sugar, Italian seasoning, salt, pepper, parsley, and Worcestershire sauce in slow cooker.

2. Cover. Cook on Low 3–4 hours, or until vegetables are soft.

3. Cool soup a bit. Puree with immersion blender.

4. Add cream and blend lightly again.

5. Serve hot with croutons and Parmesan as garnish.

TIP
This recipe can be easily doubled.

Onion Soup

Lucille Amos, Greensboro, NC

Makes 10 servings
Prep. Time: 30 minutes   Cooking Time: 4–5 hours   Ideal slow-cooker size: 4–5-qt.

6 large onions, chopped

1 stick (8 Tbsp.) butter

6 10½-oz. cans beef broth

1 ½ tsp. Worcestershire sauce

pepper, to taste

10 slices (½-inch thick) French bread

shredded mozzarella cheese and Parmesan cheese

1. In large skillet or saucepan, sauté onions in butter until tender. Do not brown. Transfer to slow cooker.

2. Add broth, Worcestershire sauce, and pepper.

3. Cover. Cook on Low 4–5 hours or until onions are very tender.

4. Divide soup between oven-safe bowls. Top each serving with French bread and cheese. Bake in a 350°F oven for 20 minutes or until cheese is melted. Remove from oven and allow to cool slightly before serving.

Broccoli, Potato, and Cheese Soup

Ruth Shank, Gridley, IL

Makes 6 servings
Prep. Time: 20–25 minutes & Cooking Time: 4 hours & Ideal slow-cooker size: 4-qt.

2 cups cubed, or diced, potatoes
3 Tbsp. chopped onions
10-oz. pkg. frozen broccoli cuts, thawed
¼ stick (2 Tbsp.) butter, melted
1 Tbsp. flour
2 cups cubed Velveeta cheese
½ tsp. salt
5½ cups milk

1. Cook potatoes and onion in boiling water in saucepan until potatoes are crisp-tender, about 10 minutes. Drain. Place in slow cooker.

2. Add remaining ingredients. Stir together.

3. Cover. Cook on Low 4 hours.

Serving Suggestion:
Serve with bread topped with bruschetta.

Matzo Ball Soup

Audrey Romonosky, Austin, TX

Makes 6 servings

Prep. Time: 30 minutes ♣ Chilling Time: 20 minutes ♣ Cooking Time: 2–6 hours ♣ Ideal slow-cooker size: 2-qt.

2 eggs
2 Tbsp. oil
2 Tbsp. water
½ cup matzo meal*
1 tsp. salt, *optional*
1 ½ qt. water
32 oz. chicken broth

1. Lightly beat eggs, oil, and 2 Tbsp. water together in a good-sized bowl.

2. Add matzo meal and salt. Mix well.

3. Cover and refrigerate 20 minutes.

4. Bring 1½ qt. water to boil in saucepan.

5. Wet hands. Roll chilled matzo mixture into 1-inch balls.

6. Drop into boiling water and cook 20 minutes. Using a slotted spoon, remove from water. Drain. (Cooked balls can be stored in refrigerator for up to 2 days.)

7. Pour chicken broth into slow cooker. Add matzo balls.

8. Cover. Cook on High 2–3 hours or on Low 5–6 hours.

*Finely crushed matzo may be substituted.

NOTE

I made this soup for an ethnic luncheon at work. Everyone enjoyed it. Matzo ball soup is traditionally served on the Jewish holiday of Passover. It is also tasty all year-round.

Hearty Bean and Vegetable Soup

Jewel Showalter, Landisville, PA

Makes 6–8 servings
Prep. Time: 20–25 minutes ⚜ *Cooking Time: 6–8 hours* ⚜ *Ideal slow-cooker size: 5-qt.*

2 medium onions, sliced
2 garlic cloves, minced
2 Tbsp. olive oil
8 cups chicken, or vegetable, broth
1 small head cabbage, chopped
2 large red potatoes, chopped
2 cups chopped celery
2 cups chopped carrots
4 cups corn
2 tsp. dried basil
1 tsp. dried marjoram
¼ tsp. dried oregano
1 tsp. salt
½ tsp. pepper
2 15-oz. cans navy beans, drained

1. Sauté onions and garlic in oil in skillet. Transfer to large slow cooker.

2. Add remaining ingredients. Mix together well.

3. Cover. Cook on Low 6–8 hours.

Variation:

Add 2–3 cups cooked and cut-up chicken 30 minutes before serving if you wish.

NOTE
I discovered this recipe after my husband's heart attack. It's a great nutritious soup using only a little fat.

Minestrone

Bernita Boyts, Shawnee Mission, KS

Makes 8–10 servings
Prep. Time: 15 minutes ❧ Cooking Time: 4–9 hours ❧ Ideal slow-cooker size: 3½–4-qt.

1 large onion, chopped
4 carrots, sliced
3 ribs celery, sliced
2 garlic cloves, minced
1 Tbsp. olive oil
6-oz. can tomato paste
14½-oz. can chicken, beef, or vegetable broth
24-oz. can pinto beans, undrained
10-oz. pkg. frozen green beans
2–3 cups chopped cabbage
1 medium zucchini, sliced
8 cups water
2 Tbsp. parsley
2 Tbsp. Italian spice
1 tsp. salt, or more to taste
½ tsp. pepper
¾ cup dry acini di pepe (small round pasta)
grated Parmesan, or Asiago, cheese

1. Sauté onion, carrots, celery, and garlic in oil in skillet until tender. Add to slow cooker.

2. Combine all other ingredients, except pasta and cheese, in slow cooker.

3. Cover. Cook 4–5 hours on High or 8–9 hours on Low.

4. Add pasta 1 hour before cooking is complete.

5. Top individual servings with cheese.

Split Pea Soup

Janette Anderson, Sedalia, MO

Makes 6–8 servings
Prep. Time: 20 minutes ♣ Cooking Time: 8–10 hours ♣ Ideal slow-cooker size: 5–6-qt.

1 or 2 ham hocks
1 lb. (2 cups) dry split peas
2 carrots, sliced
1 onion, diced
2 ribs celery, diced
¼ tsp. pepper
1 tsp. salt
3 potatoes, diced
1 qt. water
1 qt. chicken broth

1. Place ham hock(s) in slow cooker.

2. Add remaining ingredients and stir well.

3. Cover. Cook on Low 8–10 hours, or until ham and split peas are tender.

4. Remove ham bone. Allow to cool until it's possible to handle it.

5. Debone and cut up meat. Stir meat back into soup.

6. For creamier soup, cook an hour or so longer. Stir occasionally to prevent sticking.

Serving Suggestion
Serve with oyster crackers.

Variations:

1. Add 14½-oz. can diced tomatoes with juice in Step 2. —Holly Schwartz, Lac Du Flambeau, WI

2. Instead of ham hocks, use 1 lb. smoked kielbasa, sliced. Stir into soup in Step 2. —Nathan LeBeau, Rapid City, SD

Great Northern Bean Soup

Alice Miller, Stuarts Draft, VA

Makes 6–8 servings
Prep. Time: 15–20 minutes ♣ Cooking Time: 3 hours ♣ Ideal slow-cooker size: 3-qt.

2 1-lb. cans great northern beans, rinsed and drained

1-lb. can stewed, or diced, tomatoes, including juice

1–2 Tbsp. brown sugar

½ cup chopped green bell peppers

½ cup chopped red bell peppers

1. Put beans, tomatoes, and brown sugar into slow cooker. Stir until well mixed.

2. Cover. Cook on High 2½ hours.

3. Stir chopped red and green peppers into soup.

4. Cover. Cook on High 30 more minutes.

The Best Bean and Ham Soup

Hope Comerford, Clinton Township, MI

Makes 8–10 servings
Prep. Time: 8 minutes ⚜ *Soaking Time: 8 hours or overnight*
⚜ *Cooking Time: 8–12 hours* ⚜ *Ideal slow-cooker size: 7-qt.*

1 meaty ham bone or shank
1 lb. dry navy beans
1 cup chopped onions
2 garlic cloves, minced
1 cup chopped celery
1 cup mashed potato flakes
¼ cup chopped parsley
1 Tbsp. salt
1 tsp. pepper
1 tsp. nutmeg
1 tsp. oregano
1 tsp. basil
1 bay leaf
14–16 cups water

1. Place the ham bone in the bottom of the crock and pour all of the remaining ingredients into the crock around it, ending with the water. You'll want to make sure you've covered the ham bone with water.

2. Cover and cook on Low for 8–12 hours.

Blessing Soup

Alix Nancy Botsford, Seminole, OK

Makes 8–10 servings
Prep. Time: 20 minutes ❧ Soaking Time: 8 hours or overnight
❧ Cooking Time: 6–14 hours ❧ Ideal slow-cooker size: 4–5-qt.

2 cups mixed dried beans—10–18 different kinds, if you can find them!

2–2½ qt. water

1 cup diced ham

1 large onion, chopped

1 garlic clove, minced

juice of 1 lemon

14½-oz. can Italian tomatoes, chopped

1 medium carrot, chopped

½ cup chopped sweet red peppers

½ cup chopped celery

2 carrots, thinly sliced

1 tsp. salt

1 tsp. pepper

1. Wash beans. Discard any stones. Place in slow cooker. Cover with water and soak 8 hours or overnight.

2. Drain water off beans.

3. Add 2–2½ qt. water to drained beans. Cook on High 2 hours.

4. Combine all remaining ingredients with beans in slow cooker.

5. Add more water if necessary so that everything is just covered with water.

6. Cover. Cook on High 4–6 hours or on Low 8–12 hours, or until beans and other vegetables are tender but not mushy.

NOTE

During one January that was especially dismal, I invited many friends, most of whom didn't know each other, to my home. I put on a video about rose gardens around the world. Then I made this soup and a fresh bread crouton that could be eaten on top of the soup and tossed a large salad.

Grandma's Barley Soup

Andrea O'Neil, Fairfield, CT

Makes 10–12 servings
Prep. Time: 10 minutes ⚜ Cooking Time: 6–8 hours ⚜ Ideal slow-cooker size: 4–5-qt.

2 smoked ham hocks
4 carrots, sliced
4 potatoes, cubed
1 cup dry lima beans
1 cup tomato paste
1½–2 cups cooked barley
salt, if needed

1. Combine all ingredients in slow cooker, except salt.

2. Cover with water.

3. Cover. Simmer on Low 6–8 hours, or until both ham and beans are tender.

4. Debone ham hocks and return cut-up meat to soup.

5. Taste before serving. Add salt if needed.

TIP
If you want to reduce the amount of meat you eat, this dish is flavorful using only 1 ham hock.

Green Beans and Sausage Soup

Bernita Boyts, Shawnee Mission, KS

Makes 5–6 servings

Prep. Time: 20–25 minutes ⚜ *Cooking Time: 7–10 hours* ⚜ *Ideal slow-cooker size: 4–5-qt.*

⅓ lb. link sausage, sliced, or bulk sausage

1 medium onion, chopped

2 carrots, sliced

2 ribs celery, sliced

1 Tbsp. olive oil

5 medium potatoes, cubed

10-oz. pkg. frozen green beans

2 14½-oz. cans chicken broth

2 broth cans water

2 Tbsp. chopped fresh parsley, or 2 tsp. dried parsley

1–2 Tbsp. chopped fresh oregano, or 1–2 tsp. dried oregano

1 tsp. Italian spice

salt, to taste

pepper, to taste

1. Brown sausage in skillet. Stir frequently for even browning.

2. Remove meat from skillet and place in slow cooker. Reserve drippings.

3. Sauté onion, carrots, and celery in skillet drippings until tender.

4. Place sautéed vegetables in slow cooker, along with all remaining ingredients. Mix together well.

5. Cover. Cook on High 1–2 hours and then on Low 6–8 hours.

Variation:

If you like it hot, add ground red pepper or hot sauce just before serving, or offer to individual eaters to add to their own bowls.

Beef Barley Soup

Michelle Showalter, Bridgewater, VA

Makes 10–12 servings
Prep. Time: 15 minutes & Cooking Time: 4–10 hours & Ideal slow-cooker size: 6-qt.

1 lb. ground beef

oil, *optional*

1½ qt. water

1 qt. canned tomatoes, stewed, crushed, or whole

3 cups sliced carrots

1 cup diced celery

1 cup diced potatoes

1 cup diced onions

¾ cup quick-cooking barley

3 tsp. beef bouillon granules, or 3 beef bouillon cubes

2–3 tsp. salt

¼ tsp. pepper

1. Brown ground beef in skillet in oil if needed. Stir frequently to break up clumps of meat. When meat is no longer pink, drain off drippings.

2. Place meat in cooker, along with all other ingredients. Mix together well.

3. Cover. Cook on Low 8–10 hours or on High 4–5 hours.

Serving Suggestion:

Serve with fresh bread and cheese cubes.

Variation:

You may use pearl barley instead of quick-cooking barley. Cook it in a saucepan according to package directions, and add halfway through soup's cooking time.

Taco Soup with Corn

Suzanne Slagel, Midway, OH

Makes 6–8 servings
Prep. Time: 15 minutes & Cooking Time: 4–6 hours & Ideal slow-cooker size: 5–6-qt.

1 lb. ground beef
1 large onion, chopped
oil, *optional*
16-oz. can Mexican-style tomatoes
16-oz. can ranch-style beans
16-oz. can whole-kernel corn, undrained
16-oz. can kidney beans, undrained
16-oz. can black beans, undrained
16-oz. jar picante sauce

1. Brown meat and onion in skillet, in oil if needed. Stir frequently to break up clumps of meat. When meat is no longer pink, drain off drippings.

2. Place meat and onion in slow cooker. Add all other ingredients. Stir well.

3. Cover. Cook on Low 4–6 hours.

Serving Suggestion:
Serve with corn or tortilla chips, sour cream, and shredded cheese as toppings.

Chicken Noodle Soup

Jennifer J. Gehman, Harrisburg, PA

Makes 6–8 servings
Prep. Time: 5–10 minutes ⚜ Cooking Time: 4–8 hours ⚜ Ideal slow-cooker size: 5-qt.

2 cups uncooked cubed chicken, dark or white meat

15¼-oz. can corn, or 2 cups frozen corn

1 cup green beans, or peas*

10 cups water

10–12 chicken bouillon cubes

3 Tbsp. bacon drippings

½ pkg. dry kluski (or other very sturdy) noodles

*If using green beans, stir in during Step 1. If using peas, stir into slow cooker just 20 minutes before end of cooking time.

1. Combine all ingredients except noodles in slow cooker.

2. Cover. Cook on High 4–6 hours or on Low 6–8 hours.

3. Two hours before end of cooking time, stir in noodles.

Serving Suggestion:
 Garnish with microgreens or parsley and fresh cracked pepper. Serve with potato rolls and butter or grilled cheese sandwiches.

Turkey Frame Soup

Joyce Zuercher, Hesston, KS

Makes 6–8 servings
Prep. Time: 40 minutes ❧ Cooking Time: 3–4 hours ❧ Ideal slow-cooker size: 6-qt.

2–3 cups cooked and cut-up turkey*

3 qt. turkey broth

1 onion, diced

½–¾ tsp. salt, or to taste

16-oz. can chopped tomatoes

1 Tbsp. chicken bouillon granules

1 tsp. dried thyme

⅛ tsp. pepper

1½ tsp. dried oregano

4 cups chopped fresh vegetables—any combination of sliced celery, carrots, onions, rutabaga, broccoli, cauliflower, mushrooms, and more

1½ cups uncooked noodles

1. Place turkey, broth, onion, salt, tomatoes, bouillon granules, thyme, pepper, oregano, and vegetables into slow cooker. Stir.

2. Cover. Cook on Low 3–4 hours, or until vegetables are nearly done.

3. Fifteen to 30 minutes before serving time, stir in noodles. Cover. Cook on Low. If noodles are thin and small, they'll cook in 15 minutes or less. If heavier, they may need 30 minutes to become tender.

4. Stir well before serving.

*If you've got a big turkey frame, and you know it's got some good meaty morsels on it, here's what to do: Break it up enough to fit into your Dutch oven. Add 3 qt. water, 1 onion, quartered, and 2 tsp. salt. Cover, and simmer 1½ hours. Remove turkey bones from Dutch oven and allow to cool. Then debone and chop meat coarsely. Discard bones and skin. Strain broth. Begin with Step 1 above!

Turkey Meatball Soup

Mary Ann Lefever, Lancaster, PA

Makes 8 servings

Prep. Time: 30 minutes   ❧   Cooking Time: 8 hours   ❧   Ideal slow-cooker size: 5–6-qt.

4–5 large carrots, chopped

10 cups chicken broth

¾ lb. escarole, washed and cut into bite-sized pieces

1 lb. ground turkey, uncooked

1 medium onion, chopped

2 large eggs, beaten

½ cup Italian bread crumbs

½ cup freshly grated Parmesan, plus more for serving

1 tsp. salt

¼ tsp. pepper

1. In slow cooker, combine carrots and broth.

2. Stir in escarole.

3. Cover. Cook on Low 4 hours.

4. Combine turkey, onion, eggs, bread crumbs, ½ cup Parmesan cheese, salt, and pepper in good-sized bowl. Mix well and shape into 1-inch balls. Drop carefully into soup.

5. Cover cooker. Cook on Low 4 more hours, or just until meatballs and vegetables are cooked through.

6. Serve hot sprinkled with extra Parmesan cheese.

Variation:

If you wish, you can substitute 3 cups cut-up cooked turkey for the ground turkey meatballs.

Apple Chicken Stew

Lorraine Pflederer, Goshen, IN

Makes 4 servings
Prep. Time: 30–40 minutes ⚜ *Cooking Time: 4–5 hours* ⚜ *Ideal slow-cooker size: 5-qt.*

4 medium potatoes, cubed

4 medium carrots, sliced ¼-inch thick

1 medium red onion, halved and sliced

1 celery rib, thinly sliced

1½ tsp. salt

¾ tsp. dried thyme

½ tsp. pepper

¼–½ tsp. caraway seeds

2 lb. boneless, skinless chicken breasts, cubed

2 Tbsp. olive, or vegetable, oil

1 large tart apple, peeled and cubed

1¼ cups apple cider, or juice

1 Tbsp. cider vinegar

1 bay leaf

minced fresh parsley

1. Layer potatoes, carrots, onion, and celery into slow cooker.

2. In a small bowl, combine salt, thyme, pepper, and caraway seeds. Sprinkle half over vegetables.

3. In a skillet, sauté chicken in oil just until lightly browned.

4. Transfer chicken to slow cooker. Top with cubed apple.

5. In another small bowl, combine apple cider and vinegar. Pour over chicken and apple.

6. Sprinkle with remaining seasoning mixture. Lay bay leaf on top.

7. Cover. Cook on High 4–5 hours, or until vegetables are tender and chicken juices run clear.

8. Discard bay leaf. Stir before serving.

9. Sprinkle individual serving bowls with parsley.

Stay-in-Bed Stew

Janie Steele, Moore, OK
Judy Newman, Saint Mary's, ON, Canada

Makes 6 servings
Prep. Time: 20 minutes ⚥ Cooking Time: 5–6 hours ⚥ Ideal slow-cooker size: 3-qt.

1 lb. chuck stewing meat
1 large onion, cut in chunks
2 potatoes, peeled and diced large
4 carrots, peeled and sliced
10¾-oz. can tomato soup
½ soup can water
dash of pepper
½ tsp. salt
1 bay leaf
1 cup frozen peas

1. Put all ingredients except peas in slow cooker.

2. Cover. Cook on Low 5–6 hours, or until vegetables are as tender as you like them.

3. Add peas 30 minutes before serving.

4. Remove bay leaf before serving.

Wintertime Vegetable Chili

Maricarol Magill, Freehold, NJ

Makes 6 servings

Prep. Time: 20 minutes & Cooking Time: 6–8 hours & Ideal slow-cooker size: 6-qt.

1 medium butternut squash, peeled and cubed

2 medium carrots, peeled and diced

1 medium onion, diced

3 tsp.–3 Tbsp. chili powder, depending on how hot you like your chili

2 14-oz. cans diced tomatoes

4¼-oz. can chopped mild green chilies, drained

1 tsp. salt, *optional*

1 cup vegetable broth

2 16-oz. cans black beans, drained and rinsed

sour cream, *optional*

1. In slow cooker, layer all ingredients, except sour cream, in order given.

2. Cover. Cook on Low 6–8 hours, or until vegetables are as tender as you want.

3. Stir before serving.

4. Top individual servings with dollops of sour cream.

Serving Suggestion:

Serve with crusty French bread.

White Chili

Rebecca Plank Leichty, Harrisonburg, VA

Makes 6–8 servings
Prep. Time: 15 minutes ⚖ Cooking Time: 4–10 hours ⚖ Ideal slow-cooker size: 5-qt.

15-oz. can chickpeas, or garbanzo beans, undrained

15-oz. can small northern beans, undrained

15-oz. can pinto beans, undrained

1 qt. frozen corn, or 2 1-lb. bags frozen corn

1½ cups shredded cooked chicken

2 Tbsp. minced onions

1 red bell pepper, diced

3 tsp. minced garlic

3 tsp. ground cumin

½ tsp. salt

½ tsp. dried oregano

2 15-oz. cans chicken broth

1. Combine all ingredients in slow cooker.

2. Cover. Cook on Low 8–10 hours or on High 4–5 hours.

Serving Suggestion:
Serve with warmed tortilla chips topped with melted cheddar cheese.

Variation:
For more zip, add 2 tsp. chili powder, or one or more chopped jalapeño peppers, to Step 1.

Slow-Cooker Chili

Kay Magruder, Seminole, OK

Makes 8–10 servings
Prep. Time: 25 minutes & Cooking Time: 6–12 hours & Ideal slow-cooker size: 6-qt.

3 lb. stewing meat

2 cloves garlic, minced

¼ tsp. pepper

½ tsp. cumin

¼ tsp. dry mustard

7½-oz. can jalapeno relish

1 cup beef broth

1–1½ onions, chopped, according to your taste preference

½ tsp. salt

½ tsp. dried oregano

1 Tbsp. chili powder

7-oz. can green chilies, chopped

14½-oz. can stewed tomatoes, chopped

15-oz. can tomato sauce

2 15-oz. cans red kidney beans, rinsed and drained

2 15-oz. cans pinto beans, rinsed and drained

1. Combine all ingredients except kidney and pinto beans in slow cooker.

2. Cover. Cook on Low 10–12 hours or on High 6–7 hours. Add beans halfway through cooking time.

Serving Suggestion:
  Serve with Mexican corn bread or warm tortillas.

Our Favorite Chili

Ruth Shank, Gridley, IL

Makes 10–12 servings
Prep. Time: 20 minutes & Cooking Time: 4–10 hours & Ideal slow-cooker size: 5-qt.

1½ lb. ground beef

¼ cup chopped onions

1 rib celery, chopped

oil, *optional*

29-oz. can stewed tomatoes

2 15½-oz. cans red kidney beans, undrained

2 16-oz. cans chili beans, undrained

½ cup ketchup

1½ tsp. lemon juice

2 tsp. vinegar

1½ tsp. brown sugar

1½ tsp. salt

1 tsp. Worcestershire sauce

½ tsp. garlic powder

½ tsp. dry mustard powder

1 Tbsp. chili powder

2 6-oz. cans tomato paste

1. Brown ground beef, onions, and celery in skillet in oil if needed. Stir frequently to break up clumps of meat. When meat is no longer pink, drain off drippings.

2. Place meat and vegetables in slow cooker. Add all remaining ingredients. Mix well.

3. Cover. Cook on Low 8–10 hours or on High 4–5 hours.

Serving Suggestion:

Top with diced avocado. Serve with fresh warm corn bread and slices of Colby or Monterey Jack cheese.

Hearty Chili

Joylynn Keener, Lancaster, PA

Makes 8 servings
Prep. Time: 20–25 minutes ⚹ *Cooking Time: 8 hours* ⚹ *Ideal slow-cooker size: 5-qt.*

I onion, chopped

2 ribs celery, chopped

I lb. ground beef

oil, *optional*

2 14-oz. cans kidney beans, undrained

14-oz. can pinto beans, undrained

14-oz. can diced tomatoes

2 14-oz. cans tomato sauce

I green bell pepper, chopped

I Tbsp. sugar

I tsp. salt

I tsp. dried thyme

I tsp. dried oregano

I Tbsp. chili powder, or to taste

1. Brown onion, celery, and beef in skillet in oil if needed. Stir frequently to break up clumps of meat. When meat is no longer pink, drain off drippings.

2. Spoon meat into slow cooker. Stir in all remaining ingredients, mixing well.

3. Cover. Cook on Low 8 hours.

White Chicken Chili

Jewel Showalter, Landisville, PA

Makes 6–8 servings
Prep. Time: 25 minutes ∂ Cooking Time: 3½–5 hours ∂ Ideal slow-cooker size: 5-qt.

2 whole skinless chicken breasts

6 cups water

2 chopped onions

2 garlic cloves, minced

1 Tbsp. oil

2–4 4¼-oz. cans chopped green chilies, drained, depending on your taste preference

1–2 diced jalapeño peppers

2 tsp. ground cumin

1½ tsp. dried oregano

¼ tsp. cayenne pepper

½ tsp. salt

3-lb. can navy beans, undrained

1–2 cups shredded cheese

sour cream

salsa

1. Place chicken in slow cooker. Add 6 cups water.

2. Cover. Cook on Low 3–4 hours, or until chicken is tender but not dry.

3. Remove chicken from slow cooker. When cool enough to handle, cube and set aside.

4. Sauté onions and garlic in oil in skillet. Add chilies, jalapeño peppers, cumin, oregano, pepper, and salt. Sauté 2 minutes. Transfer to broth in slow cooker.

5. Add navy beans.

6. Cover. Cook on Low 30–60 minutes.

7. Right before serving add chicken and cheese.

8. Serve topped with sour cream and salsa.

Serving suggestion:

Corn bread and/or corn chips are good go-alongs with this chili.

Variation:

If you want to use dried beans, use 3 cups navy beans. Cover with water in saucepan, soaking overnight. In the morning, drain and cover with fresh water. Cook in saucepan over low heat, 7–8 hours, or until tender. Drain off excess moisture and stir into chicken and broth.

Pumpkin Black-Bean Turkey Chili

Rhoda Atzeff, Harrisburg, PA

Makes 10–12 servings
Prep. Time: 20 minutes   ☙   Cooking Time: 7–8 hours   ☙   Ideal slow-cooker size: 5-qt.

1 cup chopped onions
1 cup chopped yellow bell peppers
3 garlic cloves, minced
2 Tbsp. oil
1½ tsp. dried oregano
1½–2 tsp. ground cumin
2 tsp. chili powder
2 15-oz. cans black beans, rinsed and drained
2½ cups chopped cooked turkey
16-oz. can pumpkin
14½-oz. can diced tomatoes
3 cups chicken broth

1. Sauté onions, peppers, and garlic in oil in skillet for 8 minutes, or until soft.

2. Stir in oregano, cumin, and chili powder. Cook 1 minute. Transfer to slow cooker.

3. Stir in remaining ingredients.

4. Cover. Cook on Low 7–8 hours.

Serving Suggestion:
Top with roasted pumpkin seeds.

Corn and Shrimp Chowder

Naomi E. Fast, Hesston, KS

Makes 6 servings
Prep. Time: 20 minutes & Cooking Time: 3–4 hours & Ideal slow-cooker size: 3½-qt.

4 slices bacon, diced

1 cup chopped onions

2 cups diced, unpeeled red potatoes

2 10-oz. pkgs. frozen corn

1 tsp. Worcestershire sauce

½ tsp. paprika

½ tsp. salt

⅛ tsp. pepper

2 6-oz. cans shrimp

2 cups water

¼ stick (2 Tbsp.) butter

12-oz. can evaporated milk

chopped chives

1. Fry bacon in skillet until lightly crisp. Add onions to drippings and sauté until transparent. Using slotted spoon, transfer bacon and onions to slow cooker.

2. Add remaining ingredients to cooker, except milk and chives. Stir together well.

3. Cover. Cook on Low 3–4 hours.

4. Add milk and chives 30 minutes before end of cooking time.

Serving Suggestion:

Serve with broccoli salad.

Variation:

I frequently use frozen hash brown potatoes for speedy preparation. There is no difference in the taste.

NOTE

I learned to make this recipe in a seventh-grade home economics class. It made an impression on my father who liked seafood very much. The recipe calls for canned shrimp, but I often increase the taste appeal with extra cooked shrimp.

Main Dishes

Slow-Cooked Short Ribs

Jean A. Shaner, York, PA
Barbara L. McGinnis, Jupiter, FL

Makes 12 servings

Prep. Time: 35 minutes ❧ Cooking Time: 9–10 hours ❧ Ideal slow-cooker size: 6-qt.

⅔ cup flour

2 tsp. salt

½ tsp. pepper

4–4½ lb. boneless beef short ribs, or
6–7 lb. bone-in beef short ribs

oil, or butter

1 large onion, chopped

1½ cups beef broth

¾ cup wine, or cider vinegar

½–¾ cup packed brown sugar,
according to your taste preference

½ cup chili sauce

⅓ cup ketchup

⅓ cup Worcestershire sauce

5 garlic cloves, minced

1½ tsp. chili powder

1. Combine flour, salt, and pepper in plastic bag. Add ribs, a few at a time, and shake to coat.

2. Brown meat in small amount of oil, or butter, in batches in skillet. Transfer to slow cooker. Reserve drippings in skillet.

3. Combine remaining ingredients in skillet. Cook, stirring up browned drippings, until mixture comes to a boil. Pour over ribs.

4. Cover. Cook on Low 9–10 hours.

5. Debone and serve.

Serving Suggestion:
Serve over rice or noodles.

TIP

It is ideal to cook these ribs one day in advance of serving. Refrigerate for several hours or overnight. Remove layer of congealed fat before serving.

Cranberry Brisket

Roseann Wilson, Albuquerque, NM

Makes 5–6 servings
Prep. Time: 10–15 minutes   ♣   Cooking Time: 8–10 hours   ♣   Ideal slow-cooker size: 5-qt.

2½-lb. beef brisket
½ tsp. salt
¼ tsp. pepper
16-oz. can whole berry cranberry sauce
8-oz. can tomato sauce
½ cup chopped onions
1 Tbsp. prepared mustard

1. Rub brisket with salt and pepper. Place in slow cooker.

2. Combine cranberry sauce, tomato sauce, onions, and mustard in a mixing bowl. Spoon over brisket, being careful not to disturb seasoning on meat.

3. Cover. Cook on Low 8–10 hours, or until meat is tender but not dry.

4. Remove brisket. Slice thinly across grain. Skim fat from juices. Serve juices with brisket.

Italian Beef Au Jus

Carol Sherwood, Batavia, NY

Makes 8 servings
Prep. Time: 5 minutes ❧ Cooking Time: 8 hours ❧ Ideal slow-cooker size: 4–5-qt.

3–5-lb. boneless beef roast
4–5-oz. pkg. au jus mix
1 pkg. Italian salad dressing mix
14½-oz. can beef broth
½ soup can water

1. Place beef in slow cooker.

2. Combine remaining ingredients in bowl. Pour over roast.

3. Cover. Cook on Low 8 hours.

TIP

To thicken broth, mix 3 Tbsp. cornstarch into ¼ cup cold water in small bowl. Stir until smooth. Remove ½ cup beef broth from cooker and blend into cornstarch mixture. Stir back into broth in cooker, stirring until smooth. Cook 10–15 minutes on High until broth reaches gravy consistency.

Serving Suggestion:
Slice meat and spoon onto hard rolls with straining spoon to make sandwiches. Or shred with 2 forks and serve over noodles or rice in broth thickened with flour.

Sauerbraten

Leona M. Slabaugh, Apple Creek, OH

Makes 8–10 servings
Prep. Time: 10–20 minutes ☙ Marinating Time: 8 hours or overnight
☙ Cooking Time: 5–7 hours ☙ Ideal slow-cooker size: 6-qt.

I cup cider vinegar
¾ cup red wine vinegar
2 tsp. salt
½ tsp. black pepper
6 whole cloves
2 bay leaves
I Tbsp. mustard seeds
3½-lb. boneless top round roast, tied
20 gingersnaps (about 5 oz.), crushed

1. Combine vinegars, salt, pepper, cloves, bay leaves, and mustard seeds in a large bowl.

2. Place roast in bowl. Spoon marinade over it.

3. Cover roast in marinade and refrigerate overnight, turning once.

4. Place roast and marinade in slow cooker.

5. Cover. Cook on High 5 hours or on Low 7 hours, or until meat is tender but not dry.

6. Remove roast to platter and keep warm.

7. Strain liquid from slow cooker. Stir crushed gingersnaps into liquid until well blended.

8. Slice roast and serve with sauce alongside.

Beef Burgundy

Joyce Kaut, Rochester, NY

Makes 6 servings
Prep. Time: 30 minutes   ❧   Cooking Time: 3½–4½ hours   ❧   Ideal slow-cooker size: 3–4-qt.

2 slices bacon, cut in squares
2 lb. sirloin tip, or round, steak, cubed
¼ cup flour
½ tsp. salt
¼ tsp. seasoning salt
¼ tsp. dried marjoram
¼ tsp. dried thyme
¼ tsp. pepper
1 garlic clove, minced
1 beef bouillon cube, crushed
1 cup Burgundy wine
¼ lb. fresh mushrooms, sliced
1–1½ cups ketchup
2 Tbsp. cornstarch, *optional*
2 Tbsp. cold water, *optional*

1. Cook bacon in skillet until crisp and browned. Remove bacon, reserving drippings.

2. Coat steak with flour and brown on all sides in bacon drippings. (Don't crowd the skillet, so the steak browns rather than steams.)

3. Combine steak, bacon drippings, bacon, seasonings and herbs, garlic, bouillon cube, and wine in slow cooker.

4. Cover. Cook on Low 4 hours (or 3 hours, if you've browned the beef well in Step 2), or until beef is just tender.

5. Stir in mushrooms and ketchup.

6. Dissolve cornstarch in water in a small bowl. Stir into slow cooker—if sauce is not as thick as you wish.

7. Cover. Cook on High 15 minutes, until sauce thickens.

Serving Suggestion:
Try serving this over noodles.

Christmas Meatloaf

Wafi Brandt, Manheim, PA

Makes 4–6 servings

Prep. Time: 25 minutes   ♣   Cooking Time: 4 hours   ♣   Ideal slow-cooker size: 4-qt.

Meatloaf

2 eggs

1 envelope dry onion soup mix

½ cup seasoned bread crumbs

¼ cup chopped dried cranberries

1 tsp. parsley

1½ lb. ground beef

Sauce:

16-oz. can whole berry cranberry sauce

¾ cup ketchup

½ cup beef broth

3 Tbsp. brown sugar

3 Tbsp. finely chopped onions

2 tsp. cider vinegar

1. Mix all meatloaf ingredients together in a good-sized bowl. Shape into loaf and place in lightly greased slow cooker.

2. Mix sauce ingredients together in another bowl. Pour over meat.

3. Cover. Cook on High 4 hours.

4. Allow to stand 10 minutes before lifting out of cooker and slicing.

TIP

from Tester

After slicing and arranging the meatloaf on a platter, I ladled the sauce over the slices. There was more sauce than fit on the platter, so I put the remainder in a dish to pass. Then individuals could add more to their slices as a condiment. We loved it!

Now That's Lasagna

Shirley Unternahrer, Wayland, IA

Makes 10 servings
Prep. Time: 20 minutes ❧ Cooking Time: 4 hours ❧ Ideal slow-cooker size: 6-qt.

1 lb. sausage, or ground beef (if ground beef, add 1 tsp. dried basil, ½ tsp. salt, and ¼ tsp. pepper)

1 small onion, chopped

1 small bell pepper, chopped

1 qt. tomato juice, *divided*

15 lasagna noodles, uncooked, *divided*

12 oz. cottage cheese, *divided*

3 cups grated mozzarella cheese, *divided*

28-oz. jar spaghetti sauce of your choice, *divided*

6 oz. sliced pepperoni

3 cups grated mozzarella cheese

1. Brown sausage or beef in skillet. Drain off half the drippings. Add chopped onion and peppers to skillet. Sauté 3 minutes in drippings with meat.

2. Pour 1 cup tomato juice into slow cooker as first layer.

3. Add a layer of 5 uncooked lasagna noodles. Break to fit inside curved edges of slow cooker.

4. Spread with half of cottage cheese as next layer. Spoon half of meat/veggie mix over cottage cheese. Sprinkle with 1 cup mozzarella cheese. Spoon half of spaghetti sauce over grated cheese.

5. Add another layer of 5 lasagna noodles. Add remaining cottage cheese, followed by a layer of remaining meat/veggie mix. Add remaining 5 noodles.

6. Top with pepperoni slices, remaining spaghetti sauce, and half of remaining mozzarella cheese. Pour rest of tomato juice slowly around edge of cooker and its ingredients.

7. Cover. Cook on High 3½ hours. Remove lid and top with remaining mozzarella cheese. Cook another 15 minutes.

8 Allow lasagna to rest 15–20 minutes before serving.

Potluck Beef Barbecue Sandwiches

Carol Sommers, Millersburg, OH

Makes 16 servings

Prep. Time: 5–10 minutes ☙ Cooking Time: 6½–8¾ hours ☙ Ideal slow-cooker size: 5-qt.

4-lb. beef chuck roast
1 cup brewed coffee, or water
1 Tbsp. apple cider, or red wine, vinegar
1 tsp. salt
½ tsp. pepper
14-oz. bottle ketchup
15-oz. can tomato sauce
1 cup sweet pickle relish
2 Tbsp. Worcestershire sauce
¼ cup brown sugar

1. Place roast, coffee, vinegar, salt, and pepper in slow cooker.

2. Cover. Cook on High 6–8 hours, or until meat is very tender.

3. Pour off cooking liquid. Shred meat with two forks.

4. Add remaining ingredients. Stir well.

5. Cover. Cook on High 30–45 minutes. Reduce heat to Low for serving.

Spanish Stuffed Peppers

Katrine Rose, Woodbridge, VA

Makes 4 servings
Prep. Time: 20 minutes   ♣   Cooking Time: 8–10 hours   ♣   Ideal slow-cooker size: 6–7-qt.

1 lb. ground beef

7-oz. pkg. Spanish rice mix

1 egg

¼ cup chopped onions

4 medium-sized green bell peppers, halved lengthwise, cored, and seeded

28-oz. can stewed, or crushed, tomatoes

10¾-oz. can tomato soup

1 cup water

shredded cheese, *optional*

1. Combine beef, rice mix (reserving seasoning packet), egg, and onions in large bowl.

2. Divide meat mixture among pepper halves.

3. Pour tomatoes into slow cooker. Arrange pepper halves over tomatoes.

4. Combine tomato soup, rice-mix seasoning packet, and water in bowl. Pour over peppers.

5. Cover. Cook on Low 8–10 hours.

6. Twenty minutes before end of the cooking time, top stuffed peppers with cheese if you wish.

Barbecued Ribs

Virginia Bender, Dover, DE

Makes 6 servings
Prep. Time: 10 minutes ⚜ Cooking Time: 8–10 hours ⚜ Ideal slow-cooker size: 6-qt.

4 lb. pork ribs
½ cup brown sugar
12-oz. jar chili sauce
¼ cup balsamic vinegar
2 Tbsp. Worcestershire sauce
2 Tbsp. Dijon mustard
1 tsp. hot sauce

1. Place ribs in slow cooker.

2. Combine remaining ingredients in a good-sized bowl.

3. Pour half of sauce over ribs.

4. Cover. Cook on Low 8–10 hours.

5. Serve with remaining sauce.

Autumn Harvest Pork Loin

Stacy Schmucker Stoltzfus, Enola, PA

Makes 4–6 servings
Prep. Time: 30 minutes & Cooking Time: 5–6 hours & Ideal slow-cooker size: 5-qt.

1 cup cider, or apple juice

1½–2-lb. pork loin

salt

pepper

2 large Granny Smith apples, peeled and sliced

1½ whole butternut squash, peeled and cubed

½ cup brown sugar

¼ tsp. cinnamon

¼ tsp. dried thyme

¼ tsp. dried sage

1. Heat cider in hot skillet. Sear pork loin on all sides in cider.

2. Sprinkle meat with salt and pepper on all sides. Place in slow cooker, along with pan juices.

3. In a good-sized bowl, combine apples and squash. Sprinkle with sugar and herbs. Stir. Spoon around pork loin in cooker.

4. Cover. Cook on Low 5–6 hours.

5. Remove pork from cooker. Let stand 10–15 minutes. Slice into ½-inch-thick slices.

6. Serve topped with apples and squash.

Cranberry Pork Loin

Barbara Walker, Sturgis, SD
Donna Treloar, Muncie, IN

Makes 9–12 servings
Prep. Time: 15 minutes   Cooking Time: 6¼–8¼ hours   Ideal slow-cooker size: 5-qt.

3–4-lb. boneless rolled pork loin roast
2 Tbsp. canola oil
14-oz. can whole berry cranberry sauce
¾ cup sugar
¾ cup cranberry juice
1 tsp. ground mustard
1 tsp. pepper
¼ tsp. ground cloves
¼ cup cornstarch
¼ cup cold water
salt, to taste

1. In Dutch oven, brown roast in oil on all sides over medium-high heat. You may need to cut roast in half to fit into your Dutch oven and/or your slow cooker.

2. Place browned roast in slow cooker.

3. In a medium-sized bowl, combine cranberry sauce, sugar, cranberry juice, mustard, pepper, and cloves. Pour over roast.

4. Cover. Cook on Low 6–8 hours, or until a meat thermometer reads 160°F in center of roast. Remove roast and keep warm. Keep sauce on Low in slow cooker.

5. In a small bowl, combine cornstarch, water, and salt until smooth.

6. Turn cooker to High. Stir cornstarch-water mixture into cooking juices. Bring to a boil. Cook and stir until sauce thickens. Serve with slices of pork roast.

Variations:

1. In place of sugar, use ¼ cup honey.

2. Instead of ¼ tsp. ground cloves, use ⅛ tsp. ground cloves and ⅛ tsp. ground nutmeg.

3. Add 1 tsp. grated orange peel to Step 3. —Renee Baum, Chambersburg, PA

4. Create a whole different twist to the Cranberry Pork Loin by dropping the sugar, cranberry juice, ground mustard, pepper, and cloves. Instead, add 2 Tbsp. Dijon mustard, 1 Tbsp. grated horseradish, and 1 cup chicken stock to the cranberry sauce. Continue with Steps 4–6. —Susan Kasting, Jenks, OK

Pork Loin with Spiced Fruit Sauce

Maricarol Magill, Freehold, NJ

Makes 4 servings
Prep. Time: 25–40 minutes ♣ Cooking Time: 4–6 hours ♣ Ideal slow-cooker size: 5–6-qt.

8-oz. pkg. dried mixed fruit (including plums and apricots), chopped
¼ cup golden raisins
2 tsp. minced fresh ginger
I small onion, chopped
⅓ cup brown sugar
2 Tbsp. cider vinegar
¾ cup water
¼ tsp. ground cinnamon
¼ tsp. curry powder
½ tsp. salt, *divided*
½ tsp. pepper, *divided*
2¼-lb. boneless pork loin roast, trimmed of fat
3/4 lb. fresh green beans, ends nipped off
I Tbsp. Dijon mustard
I Tbsp. cornstarch
I Tbsp. cold water

1. In slow cooker, combine dried mixed fruit, raisins, ginger, onion, sugar, vinegar, water, cinnamon, curry powder, and ¼ tsp. each of salt and pepper. Stir.

2. Season pork with remaining ¼ tsp. salt and pepper. Place pork on top of fruit mixture in slow cooker. Cover. Cook on High 2 hours or on Low 3 hours.

3. Layer green beans over pork. Cover.

4. Cook for 2 more hours on High or for 3 more hours on Low—or until meat is tender and beans are done to your liking.

5. When meat and beans are tender but not dry, remove to separate plates. Cover and keep warm.

6. Stir mustard into sauce in cooker.

7. In a small bowl, mix cornstarch with 1 Tbsp. cold water until smooth. Stir into sauce.

8. Cover. Turn cooker to High and let sauce cook a few minutes until thickened.

9. Slice pork and serve with sauce and green beans.

NOTE

We discovered this to be a great Christmas dinner one year when we were remodeling and had limited kitchen facilities. I put the ingredients in the slow cooker, and we played Scrabble all day while it cooked. I served it with microwaved rice pilaf. It was my most stress-free Christmas ever!

Oxford Canal Chops Deluxe

Willard E. Roth, Elkhart, IN

Makes 6 servings
Prep. Time: 25 minutes   Cooking Time: 4 hours   Ideal slow-cooker size: 5-qt.

6 6-oz. boneless pork chops
¼ cup flour
1 tsp. powdered garlic
1 tsp. sea salt
1 tsp. black pepper
1 tsp. dried basil and/or dried oregano
2 medium onions, sliced
2 Tbsp. oil
1 cup Burgundy wine
14½-oz. can beef broth
1 soup can water
6-oz. can tomato sauce
8 oz. dried apricots
½ lb. fresh mushroom caps or sliced mushrooms

1. Shake chops in bag with flour and seasonings.

2. Glaze onions in oil in medium hot skillet. Add chops and brown on both sides.

3. Pour any remaining flour over chops in skillet.

4. In large bowl mix together wine, broth, water, and tomato sauce. Pour over meat. Bring to boil.

5. Remove chops from skillet and place in cooker.

6. Layer in apricots and mushrooms. Pour heated broth over top.

7. Cover. Cook on Low 2½ hours, and then on High 1½ hours, or until chops are just tender.

Serving Suggestion:
This is a great dish to serve with the Celtic speciality Bubble and Squeak—Irish potatoes mashed with green cabbage or Brussels sprouts.

NOTE
My favorite memory with this recipe was the time I prepared it in the tiny kitchen of a houseboat on the Oxford Canal and then shared it with five friends. It was a hit!

Italian Sausage

Lauren Eberhard, Seneca, IL

Makes 15 servings
Prep. Time: 40 minutes   ♣   Cooking Time: 6–7 hours   ♣   Ideal slow-cooker size: 6-qt., or 2 4-qt. cookers

5 lb. Italian sausage in casing

4 large green bell peppers, sliced

3 large onions, sliced

1–2 garlic cloves, minced

28-oz. can tomato puree

14-oz. can tomato sauce

12-oz. can tomato paste

1 Tbsp. dried oregano

1 Tbsp. dried basil

½ tsp. garlic powder

1½ tsp. salt

2 tsp. sugar

1. Cut sausage into 4- or 5-inch pieces and brown on all sides in batches in skillet.

2. Sauté peppers, onions, and garlic in drippings.

3. Combine tomato puree, sauce, and paste in bowl. Stir in seasonings and sugar.

4. Layer half of sausage, onions, and peppers in 6-qt. slow cooker, or in 2 4-qt. cookers. Cover with half the tomato mixture. Repeat layers.

5. Cover. Cook on High 1 hour and then on Low 5–6 hours.

Serving suggestion:
Serve over pasta, or dip mixture with a straining spoon onto Italian sandwich rolls.

Kielbasa and Cabbage

Mary Ann Lefever, Lancaster, PA

Makes 4 servings
Prep. Time: 10–15 minutes & *Cooking Time: 8 hours* & *Ideal slow-cooker size: 4–5-qt.*

I lb. kielbasa, cut into 4 chunks

4 large white potatoes, cut into chunks

1-lb. head green cabbage, shredded

I qt. whole tomatoes (strained if you don't like seeds)

onion, thinly sliced, *optional*

1. Layer kielbasa, then potatoes, and then cabbage into slow cooker.

2. Pour tomatoes over top.

3. Top with sliced onions if you wish.

4. Cover. Cook on High 8 hours, or until meat is cooked through and vegetables are as tender as you like them.

TIP
If desired, brown kielbasa in a skillet over medium heat before adding to slow cooker.

Brown Sugar and Honey Ham

Hope Comerford, Clinton Township, MI

Makes 18 servings
Prep. Time: 5 minutes ❧ Cooking Time: 4 hours ❧ Ideal slow-cooker size: 6-qt.

1–1½ cups brown sugar
½ tsp. ground clove
1 6–8 lb. boneless spiral ham
2–3 Tbsp. honey

1. Mix together the brown sugar and ground clove. Place ¼ cup of this mixture into the bottom of your crock and spread it around a bit.

2. Place the spiral ham, non-skin side down, on top of the brown sugar mixture in the crock.

3. Drizzle the honey over the ham. Press the rest of the brown sugar mixture onto the ham, creating a brown sugar crust.

4. Cover and cook on Low for 4 hours.

Ham with Pineapple Sauce

Kayla Snyder, North East, PA

Makes 14–16 servings
Prep. Time: 20–30 minutes ⚜ Cooking Time: 3 hours ⚜ Ideal slow-cooker size: 5-qt.

20-oz. can crushed pineapple, undrained

1 tsp. vinegar

1 Tbsp. lemon juice

½ tsp. salt

2 cups brown sugar

¾ tsp. dry mustard

4 Tbsp. flour

7–8-lb. ham, precooked and sliced in ¼-inch-thick slices

1. Mix together pineapple, vinegar, lemon juice, salt, brown sugar, mustard, and flour in a saucepan. Bring to boil. Cook, stirring frequently, until slightly thickened.

2. Layer several slices of ham into slow cooker. Ladle some of sauce over top of each slice. Continue layering until all ham and sauce are stacked in slow cooker.

3. Cover. Cook on High 3 hours, or until heated through.

NOTE
We served this recipe at our wedding, so it is especially special to us.

Ham with Sweet Potatoes and Oranges

Esther Becker, Gordonville, PA

Makes 4 servings

Prep. Time: 15 minutes ⚓ Cooking Time: 7–8 hours ⚓ Ideal slow-cooker size: 3-qt.

2–3 sweet potatoes, peeled and sliced ¼-inch thick

1 large ham slice

3 seedless oranges, peeled and sliced

3 Tbsp. orange juice concentrate

3 Tbsp. honey

½ cup brown sugar

2 Tbsp. cornstarch

1. Place sweet potato slices in slow cooker.

2. Arrange ham and orange slices on top of sweet potatoes.

3. Combine remaining ingredients in a small bowl. Drizzle over ham and oranges.

4. Cover. Cook on Low 7–8 hours.

Serving Suggestion:

Delicious served with a fruit salad.

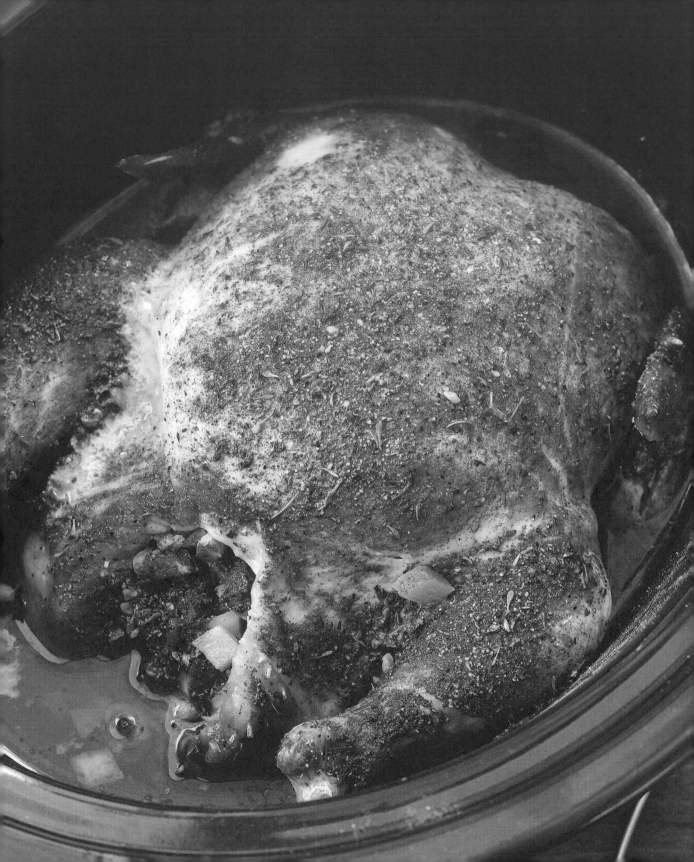

Sunday Roast Chicken

Ruth A. Feister, Narvon, PA

Makes 4–5 servings

Prep. Time: 30–35 minutes ⚭ Cooking Time: 6 hours ⚭ Ideal slow-cooker size: 6–7-qt.

¼ stick (2 Tbsp.) butter

2 cups chopped onions

I cup chopped green bell peppers

I roasting chicken

¼ cup flour

Seasoning Mix:

I Tbsp. salt

2 tsp. paprika

1½ tsp. onion powder

1½ tsp. garlic powder

1½ tsp. dried basil

I tsp. dry mustard

I tsp. cumin

2 tsp. pepper

½ tsp. dried thyme

½ tsp. savory

1. Combine seasoning mix ingredients in small bowl.

2. Melt butter over high heat in skillet. When butter starts to sizzle, add chopped onions and peppers, and 3 Tbsp. seasoning mix.

3. Cook until onions are golden brown. Cool.

4. Stuff cavity of chicken with cooled vegetables.

5. Sprinkle outside of chicken with 1 Tbsp. seasoning mix. Rub in well so it sticks.

6. Place chicken in large slow cooker.

7. Cover. Cook on Low 6 hours.

8. Empty vegetable stuffing and juices into saucepan. Whisk in flour and 1 cup stock from slow cooker.

9. Cook over high heat until thickened. Add more stock if you prefer a thinner gravy.

NOTE

The first time I served this dish was when we had family visiting us from Mississippi. We had a wonderful time sitting around a large table, sharing many laughs and catching up on the years since our last visit.

Our Favorite Chicken and Stuffing

Kim Stoll, Abbeville, SC

Makes 6 servings

Prep. Time: 10–15 minutes   &   Cooking Time: 3–5 hours   &   Ideal slow-cooker size: 5-qt.

6 boneless, skinless chicken breast halves

6 slices Swiss cheese

¼ cup milk

10¾-oz. can cream of mushroom, or chicken, soup

2 cups stuffing mix

1 stick (8 Tbsp.) butter, melted

1. Grease slow cooker with nonstick cooking spray.

2. Top each breast half with slice of cheese. Arrange cheese-covered chicken in slow cooker.

3. In a mixing bowl, combine milk and soup until smooth. Pour over chicken. (If you've stacked the breasts, lift the ones on top to make sure the ones on the bottom are topped with sauce, too.)

4. Pour the stuffing mix evenly over the sauced chicken, including the chicken on the bottom.

5. Drizzle with melted butter.

6. Cover and cook on high for 3 hours, or low for 5 hours, or just until the meat is tender but not dry.

Variation:

Use cornbread stuffing instead of regular stuffing mix. —Betty Moore, Plano, IL

Chicken Cacciatore

Eleanor J. Ferreira, North Chelmsford, MA

Makes 8 servings
Prep. Time: 40 minutes   ♣   Cooking Time: 4–5 hours   ♣   Ideal slow-cooker size: 6–6½-qt., or 2 4-qt. cookers

2 chickens, cut into pieces

1 cup flour

2 tsp. salt

½ tsp. pepper

olive oil

2 4-oz. cans sliced mushrooms, drained

3 medium onions, sliced

2 celery ribs, chopped

4 large green bell peppers, cut into 1-inch strips

28-oz. can tomatoes

28-oz. can tomato puree

½ tsp. dried basil

½ tsp. dried oregano

½ tsp. salt

¼ tsp. pepper

½ tsp. dried parsley

1. Shake chicken pieces, one at a time, in bag with flour, salt, and pepper. When well coated, brown chicken pieces on both sides in skillet in oil.

2. Place chicken in large slow cooker, or in two medium-sized cookers, reserving drippings.

3. Sauté mushrooms, onions, celery, and peppers in drippings from chicken. Spread over chicken in cooker.

4. Mix remaining ingredients together in bowl and pour over chicken and vegetables.

5. Cover. Cook on Low 4–5 hours.

Serving Suggestion:
Serve over hot spaghetti.

Elegant Chicken with Gravy

Leesa Lesenski, South Deerfield, MA

Makes 6 servings
Prep. Time: 10 minutes & Cooking Time: 3–6 hours & Ideal slow-cooker size: 4-qt.

6 boneless, skinless chicken breast halves

10¾-oz. can cream of broccoli, or broccoli cheese, soup

10¾-oz. can cream of chicken soup

½ cup white wine

4-oz. can sliced mushrooms, undrained, *optional*

1. Arrange chicken breasts in slow cooker.

2. In bowl mix together soups, wine, and mushroom slices if you wish.

3. Pour over chicken.

4. Cover. Cook on High 3 hours or on Low 6 hours, or until chicken is tender but not dry.

Serving Suggestion:
Serve over rice or noodles.

Slow Cooker Creamy Italian Chicken

Sherri Grindle, Goshen, IN

Makes 8 servings
Prep. Time: 10–15 minutes & Cooking Time: 5–6 hours & Ideal slow-cooker size: 4–5-qt.

8 boneless, skinless chicken breast halves

I envelope dry Italian salad dressing mix

¼ cup water

8-oz. pkg. cream cheese, softened

10¾-oz. can cream of chicken soup

4-oz. can mushrooms, drained

1. Place chicken in greased slow cooker.

2. Combine salad dressing mix and water in bowl. Pour over chicken.

3. Cover. Cook on Low 4–5 hours.

4. In saucepan, combine cream cheese and soup. Heat slightly to melt cream cheese. Stir in mushrooms. Pour over chicken.

5. Cover. Cook 1 additional hour on Low.

Serving Suggestion:
Serve over noodles or rice.

Variation:
Add frozen vegetables along with the mushrooms in Step 4.

Chicken and Dumplings

Bonnie Miller, Louisville, OH

Makes 4 servings
Prep. Time: 20 minutes 🌢 Cooking Time: 3½–8½ hours 🌢 Ideal slow-cooker size: 4-qt.

2 lb. boneless, skinless chicken breast halves

1¾ cups chicken broth

2 chicken bouillon cubes

2 tsp. salt

1 tsp. pepper

1 tsp. poultry seasoning

2 celery ribs, cut into 1-inch pieces

6 small carrots, cut into 1-inch chunks

Biscuits:

2 cups buttermilk biscuit mix

½ cup plus 1 Tbsp. milk

1 tsp. parsley

1. Arrange chicken in slow cooker.

2. Dissolve bouillon in broth in bowl. Stir in salt, pepper, and poultry seasoning.

3. Pour over chicken.

4. Spread celery and carrots over top.

5. Cover. Cook on Low 6–8 hours or on High 3–3½ hours, or until chicken is tender but not dry.

6. Combine biscuit ingredients in a bowl until just moistened. Drop by spoonfuls over steaming chicken.

7. Cover. Cook on High 35 minutes. Do not remove cover while dumplings are cooking. Serve immediately.

Chicken Broccoli Rice Casserole

Gloria Julien, Gladstone, MI

Makes 4–6 servings
Prep. Time: 30 minutes & Cooking Time: 2–3 hours & Ideal slow-cooker size: 5-qt.

1 onion, chopped

3 Tbsp. oil

2–3 cups uncooked chicken, cut in 1-inch pieces

10¾-oz. can cream of chicken soup

12-oz. can evaporated milk

2 cups cubed Velveeta cheese

3 cups cooked rice

2 cups frozen broccoli cuts, thawed

¼ tsp. pepper

4-oz. can mushrooms, drained

1. Sauté onion in oil in skillet.

2. Add chicken and sauté until no longer pink.

3. Combine all ingredients in slow cooker.

4. Cover. Cook on Low 2–3 hours.

NOTE

1. This is an ideal dish for people who are not big meat-eaters.

2. This is good carry-in for potluck or fellowship meals. I put the ingredients together the night before.

Traditional Turkey Breast

Hope Comerford, Clinton Township, MI

Makes 6 servings
Prep. Time: 10 minutes   ⚜   Cooking Time: 8 hours   ⚜   Ideal slow-cooker size: 6½-qt.

7 lb. or less turkey breast

olive oil

½ stick butter, cut into lots of squares

Rub:

2 tsp. garlic powder

1 tsp. onion powder

1 tsp. salt

¼ tsp. pepper

1 tsp. poultry seasoning

1. Remove the gizzards from the turkey breast, rinse it and pat it dry. Place it into the bottom of the crock.

2. Mix together the rub ingredients.

3. Rub the turkey all over with olive oil, then press the rub onto the turkey breast all over.

4. Place the butter squares all over the turkey breast.

5. Cover and cook on Low for 8 hours.

Slow Cooker Turkey and Dressing

Carol Sherwood, Batavia, NY

Makes 4–6 servings

Prep. Time: 10–15 minutes   Cooking Time: 5–6 hours   Ideal slow-cooker size: 5–6-qt.

8-oz. pkg., or 2 6-oz. pkgs., stuffing mix
½ cup hot water
¼ stick (2 Tbsp.) butter, softened
1 onion, chopped
½ cup chopped celery
¼ cup dried cranberries
3-lb. boneless turkey breast
¼ tsp. dried basil
½ tsp. salt
½ tsp. pepper

1. Spread dry stuffing mix in greased slow cooker.

2. Add water, butter, onion, celery, and cranberries. Mix well.

3. Sprinkle turkey breast with basil, salt, and pepper. Place over stuffing mixture.

4. Cover. Cook on Low 5–6 hours, or until turkey is done but not dry.

5. Remove turkey. Slice and set aside.

6. Gently stir stuffing and allow to stand 5 minutes before serving.

7. Place stuffing on platter, topped with sliced turkey.

Turkey Thighs, Acorn Squash, and Apples

Mary E. Wheatley, Mashpee, MA

Makes 6–8 servings
Prep. Time: 35 minutes ⚹ *Cooking Time: 6–8 hours* ⚹ *Ideal slow-cooker size: 6-qt.*

2 lb. acorn squash, peeled, seeded, and cut into 1-inch-thick rings

6 medium-sized Granny Smith, or other tart, apples cored and cut into ½-inch-thick rings

4 turkey thighs, skin and excess fat removed

salt and pepper, to taste

1 shallot, or small onion, chopped

½ cup apple juice, or cider

1 Tbsp. apple brandy

3 Tbsp. brown sugar

1 tsp. ground cinnamon

½ tsp. ground allspice

1. Spray inside of slow cooker with nonstick spray. Layer in squash, followed by apple rings.

2. Place turkey thighs on top. Sprinkle with salt and pepper, and shallot or onion.

3. In a small bowl, combine apple juice, brandy, brown sugar, cinnamon, and allspice. Pour over turkey.

4. Cover. Cook on Low 6–8 hours, or just until turkey and squash are tender.

Barbecued Turkey Cutlets

Maricarol Magill, Freehold, NJ

Makes 6–8 servings
Prep. Time: 10 minutes ❧ *Cooking Time: 3 hours* ❧ *Ideal slow-cooker size: 4–5-qt.*

6–8 (1½–2 lb.) turkey cutlets
¼ cup molasses
¼ cup cider vinegar
¼ cup ketchup
3 Tbsp. Worcestershire sauce
1 tsp. garlic salt
3 Tbsp. chopped onions
2 Tbsp. brown sugar
¼ tsp. pepper

1. Place turkey cutlets in slow cooker.

2. Combine remaining ingredients in bowl. Pour over turkey.

3. Cover. Cook on Low 3 hours.

Serving Suggestion:
Serve over white or brown rice.

Fruited Turkey and Yams

Jean M. Butzer, Batavia, NY

Makes 4 servings
Prep. Time: 30–40 minutes & Cooking Time: 3–10 hours & Ideal slow-cooker size: 5–6-qt.

¼ stick (2 Tbsp.) butter

2–3 lb. (3–4) turkey thighs, cut in half lengthwise

2 medium (2 cups) yams, or sweet potatoes, cut crosswise into ½-inch-thick slices

1 cup mixed chopped dried fruit

1 tsp. chopped garlic

½ tsp. salt

¼ tsp. pepper

¾ cup orange juice

¼ cup chopped fresh parsley

1. Melt butter in 12-inch skillet. Add turkey thighs, skin side down. Brown over medium-high heat, turning once. Drain off drippings.

2. Meanwhile, place yams in slow cooker. Top with turkey thighs.

3. Sprinkle with dried fruit, garlic, salt, and pepper.

4. Gently pour orange juice into cooker, being careful not to disturb fruit and seasonings.

5. Cover. Cook on Low 8–10 hours or on High 3–4 hours, just until turkey is tender.

6. Slice; then sprinkle with parsley before serving.

Turkey Lasagna

Rhoda Atzeff, Lancaster, PA

Makes 8–10 servings

Prep. Time: 20–30 minutes ♣ *Cooking Time: 5 hours* ♣ *Ideal slow-cooker size: 5-qt.*

1 lb. lean ground turkey

1 onion, chopped

⅛ tsp. garlic powder

2 15-oz. cans tomato sauce

6-oz. can tomato paste

½–1 tsp. salt

1 tsp. dried oregano, or ½ tsp. dried oregano and ½ tsp. dried basil

12 oz. fat-free cottage cheese

½ cup grated Parmesan cheese

12 oz. shredded nonfat mozzarella cheese

12 oz. lasagna noodles, uncooked, *divided*

1. Brown ground turkey and onion in skillet. Drain off any drippings.

2. Stir garlic powder, tomato sauce, tomato paste, salt, and herbs into browned turkey in skillet.

3. In a good-sized mixing bowl, blend together cottage cheese, Parmesan cheese, and mozzarella cheese.

4. Spoon ⅓ of meat sauce into slow cooker.

5. Add ⅓ of uncooked lasagna noodles, breaking them to fit.

6. Top with ⅓ of cheese mixture. You may have to use a knife to spread it.

7. Repeat layers two more times.

8. Cover. Cook on Low 5 hours.

9. Allow to stand 10 minutes before serving.

NOTE

I tried this on my brothers. It is a delicious dish, but I thought their raves were maybe a bit overdone. But it was a good feeling to know it pleased them. I overheard my one brother calling another brother in Virginia and telling him about it!

Lamb Chops

Shirley Sears, Tiskilwa, IL

Makes 4–6 servings
Prep. Time: 10 minutes ⚘ *Cooking Time: 4–6 hours* ⚘ *Ideal slow-cooker size: 5-qt.*

1 medium onion, sliced
1 tsp. dried oregano
½ tsp. dried thyme
½ tsp. garlic powder
¼ tsp. salt
⅛ tsp. pepper
8 loin lamb chops (1¾–2 lb.)
2 garlic cloves, minced
¼ cup water

1. Place onion in slow cooker.

2. In a small bowl, combine oregano, thyme, garlic powder, salt, and pepper. Rub over lamb chops. Place chops in slow cooker.

3. Top chops with garlic.

4. Pour water down side of cooker, so as not to disturb rub and garlic on chops.

5. Cover. Cook on Low 4–6 hours, or until chops are tender but not dry.

Venison in Sauce

Anona M. Teel, Bangor, PA

Makes 12 sandwiches

Prep. Time: 20 minutes ⚜ *Marinating Time: 8 hours* ⚜ *Cooking Time: 8–10 hours* ⚜ *Ideal slow-cooker size: 5-qt.*

3–4-lb. venison roast
½ cup vinegar
2 garlic cloves, minced
2 Tbsp. salt
cold water
oil
large onion, sliced
½ green bell pepper, sliced
2 ribs celery, sliced
1–2 garlic cloves, minced
1½–2 tsp. salt
¼ tsp. pepper
½ tsp. dried oregano
¼ cup ketchup
1 cup tomato juice

1. Place venison in a large bowl. Combine vinegar, garlic cloves, and 2 Tbsp. salt, and pour over venison. Add water until meat is covered. Marinate 8 hours.

2. Cut meat into pieces. Brown in oil in skillet. Place in slow cooker.

3. Mix remaining ingredients together and pour into cooker. Stir together well.

4. Cover. Cook on Low 8–10 hours.

5. Using two forks, pull meat apart and stir it through sauce.

Serving Suggestion:
   Serve on sandwich rolls, or over rice or pasta.

Macaroni and Cheese

Sherry L. Lapp, Lancaster, PA

Makes 8 servings
Prep. Time: 20 minutes ⚬ *Cooking Time: 3 hours* ⚬ *Ideal slow-cooker size: 4-qt.*

8-oz. pkg. elbow macaroni, cooked al dente

12-oz. can evaporated milk

1 cup whole milk

½ stick (4 Tbsp.) butter, melted

2 large eggs, slightly beaten

4 cups grated sharp cheddar cheese, *divided*

¼–½ tsp. salt, according to your taste preference

⅛ tsp. white pepper

¼ cup grated Parmesan cheese

1. In slow cooker, combine lightly cooked macaroni, evaporated milk, whole milk, melted butter, eggs, 3 cups cheddar cheese, salt, and pepper.

2. Top with remaining cheddar and Parmesan cheeses.

3. Cover. Cook on Low 3 hours.

Variations:

1. Add 12-oz. can drained tuna in Step 1. —Janice Muller, Derwood, MD

2. Add ½ tsp. paprika and 2–4 Tbsp. minced onions in Step 1. —Kaye Taylor, Florissant, MO

Side Dishes

Cranberry Orange Sauce

Hope Comerford, Clinton Township, MI

Makes 6 servings
Prep. Time: 5 minutes   Cooking Time: 4–5 hours   Ideal slow-cooker size: 1½-qt.

12-oz. bag frozen cranberries
⅓ cup sugar
4 Tbsp. orange juice
1 Tbsp. lemon juice
1 Tbsp. orange zest

1. Place the cranberries into the bottom of the crock.

2. Add in the sugar, orange juice, lemon juice, and orange zest. Stir.

3. Cover and cook on Low for 4–5 hours.

4. You can serve this hot or cold, depending on how you like it. You can also serve it chunky as is, or you can use an immersion blender and make it smooth.

Christmas Carrots

Lindsey Spencer, Marrow, OH

Makes 8 servings
Prep. Time: 10–15 minutes ⚘ Cooking Time: 3 hours ⚘ Ideal slow-cooker size: 3-qt.

2 lb. carrots
½ stick (4 Tbsp.) butter, melted
½ cup brown sugar
8-oz. can crushed pineapple, undrained
½ cup shredded coconut

1. Peel carrots and cut into strips ½ inch wide and 2 inches long.

2. For extra flavor, brown carrots in skillet in butter before placing in slow cooker. Or skip doing that and place carrots and butter straight into slow cooker.

3. Add all other ingredients, except shredded coconut, to slow cooker. Mix together gently but well.

4. Cover. Cook on Low 3 hours.

5. Add coconut as garnish to carrots when serving.

Glazed Carrots

Barbara Smith, Bedford, PA

Makes 3–4 servings
Prep. Time: 15 minutes ♣ Cooking Time: 2½–3½ hours ♣ Ideal slow-cooker size: 2½-qt.

3 cups thinly sliced carrots or baby carrots

2 cups water

¼ tsp. salt

2–3 Tbsp. butter

3 Tbsp. orange marmalade

2 Tbsp. chopped pecans, *optional*

1. Combine carrots, water, and salt in slow cooker.

2. Cover. Cook on High 2–3 hours, or until carrots are as tender as you like them.

3. Drain. Stir in butter and marmalade.

4. Cover. Cook on High 30 minutes.

Cheesy Broccoli Casserole

Dorothy VanDeest, Memphis, TN

Makes 3–4 servings
Prep. Time: 10–15 minutes ❧ Cooking Time: 3–5 hours ❧ Ideal slow-cooker size: 3-qt.

10-oz. pkg. frozen chopped broccoli
6 eggs, beaten
24 oz. small-curd cottage cheese
6 Tbsp. flour
8 oz. mild cheese of your choice, diced
½ stick (4 Tbsp.) butter, melted
2 green onions, chopped
salt, to taste

1. Place frozen broccoli in colander. Run cold water over it until it thaws. Separate into pieces. Drain well.

2. Combine broccoli and all other ingredients in greased slow cooker. Mix together gently but well.

3. Cover. Cook on High 1 hour. Stir well, then continue cooking on Low 2–4 hours.

Quick Broccoli Fix

Willard E. Roth, Elkhart, IN

Makes 6 servings
Prep. Time: 15 minutes ❧ Cooking Time: 5–6 hours ❧ Ideal slow-cooker size: 3½-qt.

1 lb. fresh, or frozen, broccoli, cut up
10¾-oz. can cream of mushroom soup
½ cup mayonnaise
½ cup plain yogurt
½ lb. sliced fresh mushrooms
1 cup shredded cheddar cheese, *divided*
1 cup crushed saltine crackers
sliced almonds, *optional*

1. Microwave broccoli for 3 minutes. Place in greased slow cooker.

2. Combine soup, mayonnaise, yogurt, mushrooms, and ½ cup cheese in mixing bowl. Pour over broccoli. Stir together gently but well.

3. Cover. Cook on Low 5–6 hours.

4. Top with remaining cheese and crackers for last half hour of cooking time.

5. If you wish, top with sliced almonds, for a special touch, before serving.

Baked Corn

Velma Stauffer, Akron, PA

Makes 8 servings
Prep. Time: 5–10 minutes   ♣   Cooking Time: 3¾ hours   ♣   Ideal slow-cooker size: 2-qt.

1 qt. fresh, or 2 1-lb. bags frozen, corn
2 eggs, beaten
1 tsp. salt
1 cup milk
⅛ tsp. pepper
2 tsp. oil
3 Tbsp. sugar
3 Tbsp. flour

1. Combine all ingredients well in greased slow cooker.

2. Cover. Cook on High 3 hours and then on Low 45 minutes.

TIP
If you use homegrown sweet corn, you could reduce the amount of sugar.

Confetti Scalloped Corn

Rhoda Atzeff, Harrisburg, PA

Makes 6–8 servings

Prep. Time: 15 minutes ❧ Cooking Time: 2–2½ hours ❧ Ideal slow-cooker size: 3-qt.

2 eggs, beaten

1 cup sour cream

½ stick (¼ cup) butter, melted

1 small onion, finely chopped, or 2 Tbsp. dried chopped onions

11-oz. can Mexican-style corn, drained

14-oz. can cream-style corn

2–3 Tbsp. green jalapeño salsa, regular salsa, or chopped green chilies

8½-oz. pkg. corn bread mix

1. Combine all ingredients in lightly greased slow cooker.

2. Cover. Bake on High 2–2½ hours, or until corn is fully cooked.

Corn Bread Casserole

Arlene Groff, Lewistown, PA

Makes 8 servings
Prep. Time: 10 minutes ❧ Cooking Time: 3¼–4 hours ❧ Ideal slow-cooker size: 3½–4-qt.

1 qt., or 2 14½-oz. cans, whole-kernel corn
1 qt., or 2 14½-oz. cans, creamed corn
1 pkg. corn muffin mix
1 egg
¼ stick (2 Tbsp.) butter
¼ tsp. garlic powder
2 Tbsp. sugar
¼ cup milk
½ tsp. salt
¼ tsp. pepper

1. Combine all ingredients in greased slow cooker.

2. Cover. Cook on Low 3½–4 hours, stirring once halfway through.

Variation:

You can replace 1 egg and ¼ cup milk with 8 oz. sour cream. —Kendra Dreps, Liberty, PA

Green Bean Casserole

Jane Meiser, Harrisonburg, VA

Makes 4 servings
Prep. Time: 10–15 minutes ❧ *Cooking Time: 3–4 hours* ❧ *Ideal slow-cooker size: 3-qt.*

14½-oz. can green beans, drained, *divided*

3½-oz. can french-fried onions, *divided*

1 cup grated cheddar cheese, *divided*

8-oz. can water chestnuts, drained, *divided*

10¾-oz. can cream of chicken soup

¼ cup white wine, or water

½ tsp. curry powder

¼ tsp. pepper

1. Alternate layers of half the beans, half the onions, half the cheese, and half the water chestnuts in slow cooker. Repeat.

2. Combine remaining ingredients in a bowl. Pour over vegetables in slow cooker.

3. Cover. Cook on Low 3–4 hours.

Baked Acorn Squash

Dale Peterson, Rapid City, SD

Makes 4 servings
Prep. Time: 15 minutes & Cooking Time: 5–6 hours
& Ideal slow-cooker size: 5–6-qt., or 2 4–6-qt., depending on size of squash

2 acorn squash
⅔ cup cracker crumbs
½ cup coarsely chopped pecans
5⅓ Tbsp. (⅓ cup) butter, melted
4 Tbsp. brown sugar
½ tsp. salt
¼ tsp. ground nutmeg
2 Tbsp. orange juice

1. Cut squash in half through the middle. Remove seeds.

2. Combine remaining ingredients in a bowl. Spoon into squash halves.

3. Place squash halves in slow cooker side by side.

4. Cover. Cook on Low 5–6 hours, or until squash is tender.

Tzimmes

Elaine Vigoda, Rochester, NY

Makes 6–8 servings
Prep. Time: 25–30 minutes   ♣   Cooking Time: 10 hours   ♣   Ideal slow-cooker size: 6-qt. or 2 4–5-qt.

1–2 sweet potatoes, sliced
6 carrots, sliced
1 potato, peeled and diced
1 onion, chopped
2 apples, peeled and sliced
1 butternut squash, peeled and sliced
¼ cup dry white wine, or apple juice
½ lb. dried apricots
1 Tbsp. ground cinnamon
1 Tbsp. apple pie spice
1 Tbsp. maple syrup, or honey
1 tsp. salt
1 tsp. ground ginger

1. Combine all ingredients in large slow cooker, or mix all ingredients in large bowl and then divide between 2 4–5-qt. cookers.

2. Cover. Cook on Low 10 hours.

NOTE

This is a special dish served primarily on Jewish holidays such as Rosh Hashanah and Passover. The sweetness of the vegetables and fruit signifies wishes for a sweet year.

Candied Sweet Potatoes

Jean M. Butzer, Batavia, NY

Makes 8 servings
Prep. Time: 5–10 minutes & Cooking Time: 2¼–3¼ hours & Ideal slow-cooker size: 5-qt.

2 29-oz. cans cut sweet potatoes, drained

½ cup chopped pecans

¾ stick (6 Tbsp.) butter, cut in pieces

2 Tbsp. frozen orange juice concentrate, thawed

⅓ cup brown sugar

2 tsp. pumpkin pie spice

½ tsp. cayenne pepper, *optional*

3 cups miniature marshmallows

1. Stir together sweet potatoes, pecans, butter, and orange juice concentrate in lightly greased slow cooker.

2. In a small bowl, combine brown sugar, pumpkin pie spice, and cayenne pepper if you wish. Sprinkle over sweet potato mixture and stir.

3. Cover. Cook on Low 2–3 hours, or until potatoes are heated through.

4. Sprinkle marshmallows over top of sweet potatoes.

5. Cover. Cook on Low 15 minutes, or until marshmallows are melted.

Decadent Sweet Potato Casserole

Hope Comerford, Clinton Township, MI

Makes 8–10 servings
Prep. Time: 10 minutes 🍂 Cooking Time: 8 hours 🍂 Ideal slow-cooker size: 6-qt.

2 apples, peeled, cored, and chopped

4–5 medium sweet potatoes, peeled and chopped

1 stick butter, melted

1 tsp. vanilla extract

½ tsp. cinnamon

½ cup brown sugar

2 cups mini marshmallows

1. In a bowl, mix together the apples and sweet potatoes.

2. In a smaller bowl, mix together the melted butter, vanilla, cinnamon, and brown sugar. Pour this over the apples and sweet potatoes and stir until everything is covered equally.

3. Spray your crock with nonstick spray, then dump the apple and sweet potato mixture into the crock.

4. Cover and cook on Low for 8 hours.

5. Five minutes before serving, sprinkle the marshmallows over the top of your casserole. Cover until the marshmallows are melted, then serve.

Sweet Potato and Cranberry Casserole

Mary E. Wheatley, Mashpee, MA

Makes 6–8 servings

Prep. Time: 20–30 minutes 🜍 Cooking Time: 3–4 hours 🜍 Ideal slow-cooker size: 4–6-qt.

¼ cup orange juice

1 stick (8 Tbsp.) butter

2–3 Tbsp. brown sugar

1 tsp. ground cinnamon

1 cup dried cranberries

salt

4 lb. sweet potatoes, or yams, peeled and cut into 1-inch pieces

1. Place all ingredients except sweet potatoes in slow cooker. Mix together.

2. Cover. Cook on High while preparing sweet potatoes.

3. Add sweet potato pieces to warm mixture.

4. Cover. Cook on High 3–4 hours.

5. When sweet potatoes are soft, stir until they're mashed and then serve.

Make-Ahead Mixed Potatoes Florentine

Becky Frey, Lebanon, PA

Makes 10–12 servings

Prep. Time: 45–60 minutes ⚜ Cooking Time: 8–10 hours ⚜ Ideal slow-cooker size: 4-qt.

6 medium-sized white potatoes

3 medium-sized sweet potatoes

1 large onion, chopped

1–2 cloves garlic, pressed

¼ stick (2 Tbsp.) butter

2 Tbsp. olive oil

8 oz. low-fat, or nonfat, cream cheese, at room temperature

½ cup nonfat sour cream

½ cup nonfat plain yogurt

1 tsp. salt, or to taste

1–1½ tsp. dill weed

¼ tsp. black pepper

10-oz. pkg. frozen, chopped spinach, thawed and squeezed dry

Variation:

You can use 1 cup plain yogurt and omit the sour cream, or vice versa. The more yogurt, the greater the savory tang.

1. Peel and quarter both white and sweet potatoes. Place in slow cooker. Barely cover with water.

2. Cover. Cook on Low 6–8 hours, or until potatoes are falling-apart tender.

3. Meanwhile, in a saucepan, sauté onion and garlic in butter and olive oil on low heat, until soft and golden.

4. In an electric mixer bowl, combine sautéed onion and garlic with cream cheese, sour cream, yogurt, salt, dill weed, and pepper. Whip until well blended. Set aside.

5. Drain off some of the potato cooking water, but reserve. Mash potatoes in some of their cooking water until soft and creamy. Add more cooking water if you'd like a creamier result.

6. Stir onion and cheese mixture into mashed potatoes.

7. Fold spinach into potato mixture.

8. Turn into greased 4-qt. slow cooker. Cook for 2 hours on Low, or until heated through.

9. If you've made the potatoes a day or so in advance of serving them, refrigerate them until the day of your gathering. Then heat potatoes in slow cooker for 3–4 hours on Low, or until heated through.

Creamy Chive and Onion Mashed Potatoes

Hope Comerford, Clinton Township, MI

Makes 6–8 servings
Prep. Time: 15 minutes ⚜ Cooking Time: 3–4 hours ⚜ Ideal slow-cooker size: 3-qt

4 lb. potatoes, peeled and cubed

2 chicken bouillon cubes

6 cups water

4 Tbsp. butter

¼–½ cup milk

8 oz. chive and onion cream cheese

1½–2 tsp. salt

⅛ tsp. pepper

1. Place the potatoes and bouillon cubes into the crock. Cover them with the water.

2. Cover and cook on Low for 3–4 hours, or until the potatoes are tender.

3. Drain the potatoes in a colander and rinse out your crock with HOT water. (Using cold water may cause it to crack.)

4. Place the potatoes back into the crock with the butter, milk, cream cheese, salt, and pepper.

5. Use a potato masher to mash the potatoes, or an immersion blender to make them smooth. You may need to add more milk depending on what consistency you like.

Creamy Red Potatoes

Kayla Snyder, North East, PA

Makes 8 servings
Prep. Time: 20–30 minutes   ⚜   Cooking Time: 3½ hours   ⚜   Ideal slow-cooker size: 3-qt.

3 Tbsp. butter

3 Tbsp. flour

1 cup milk

½ tsp. garlic powder

¾ tsp. salt

1 Tbsp. dried onion flakes

1 tsp. parsley flakes

2 3-oz. pkgs. cream cheese, at room temperature

2 lb. red potatoes

1. Make a white sauce in a saucepan by melting butter, stirring in flour, and adding milk. Whisk until smooth and thickened.

2. Add seasonings. Beat in cream cheese until smooth.

3. Cut unpeeled potatoes into 1–2-inch cubes.

4. Layer potatoes and sauce in slow cooker.

5. Cover. Cook on High 3½ hours, or until potatoes are as soft as you like them.

TIP

1. 1½ lb. of potatoes fills up a 3-qt. slow cooker nicely.

2. Mix up the sauce ahead of time and refrigerate it. Then when you're ready, cut up the potatoes, and put them and the sauce in your slow cooker.

Herbed Potatoes

Jo Haberkamp, Fairbank, IA

Makes 6 servings
Prep. Time: 10 minutes ❧ Cooking Time: 2½–3 hours ❧ Ideal slow-cooker size: 3-qt.

1½ lb. small new potatoes

¼ cup water

½ stick (4 Tbsp.) butter, melted

3 Tbsp. chopped fresh parsley

1 Tbsp. lemon juice

1 Tbsp. chopped fresh chives

1 Tbsp. dill weed

¼–½ tsp. salt, according to your taste preference

⅛–¼ tsp. pepper, according to your taste preference

1. Wash potatoes. Peel a strip around the middle of each potato. Place prepared potatoes in slow cooker.

2. Add water.

3. Cover. Cook on High 2½–3 hours. Drain well.

4. In saucepan, heat butter, parsley, lemon juice, chives, dill weed, salt, and pepper.

5. Pour sauce over potatoes.

Serving Suggestion:
Serve with ham or any meat dish
that does not make its own gravy.

Pete's Scalloped Potatoes

Dede Peterson, Rapid City, SD

Makes 8–10 servings
Prep. Time: 15 minutes & Cooking Time: 6–7 hours & Ideal slow-cooker size: 6-qt.

5 lb. red potatoes, peeled or unpeeled and sliced, *divided*

2 cups water

1 tsp. cream of tartar

¼ lb. bacon, cut in 1-inch squares, browned until crisp, and drained, *divided*

dash of salt

½ pt. whipping cream

1 pt. half-and-half

1. In large bowl, toss sliced potatoes in water and cream of tartar. Drain.

2. Layer half of potatoes and half of bacon in large slow cooker. Sprinkle each layer with salt.

3. Repeat layers using all remaining potatoes and bacon.

4. Mix whipping cream and half-and-half in bowl. Pour over potatoes.

5. Cover. Cook on Low 6–7 hours.

Variation:

For added flavor, cut one large onion into thin rings. Sauté in bacon drippings, and then layer onion along with potatoes and bacon in slow cooker. Sprinkle each layer of potatoes with salt and pepper. Continue with Step 4.

Cheese Potatoes

Joyce Shackelford, Green Bay, WI

Makes 10 servings
Prep. Time: 10–15 minutes & Cooking Time: 8¼ hours & Ideal slow-cooker size: 5-qt.

6 potatoes, peeled and cut into ¼-inch strips

2 cups shredded sharp cheddar cheese

10¾-oz. can cream of chicken soup

1 small onion, chopped

½ stick (4 Tbsp.) butter, melted

1 tsp. salt

1 tsp. pepper

1 cup sour cream

2 cups seasoned stuffing cubes

3 Tbsp. butter, melted

1. Toss together potatoes and cheese in slow cooker.

2. In a bowl, combine soup, onion, 4 Tbsp. melted butter, salt, and pepper. Pour over potatoes. Mix together gently.

3. Cover. Cook on Low 8 hours.

4. Stir in sour cream. Cover and heat 10 more minutes.

5. Meanwhile, toss together stuffing cubes and 3 Tbsp. melted butter in bowl. Sprinkle over potatoes just before serving.

Hot German Potato Salad

Judi Manos, West Islip, NY

Makes 6 servings
Prep. Time: 15 minutes & Cooking Time: 8–10 hours & Ideal slow-cooker size: 3-qt.

5 medium-sized potatoes, cut ¼-inch thick

1 large onion, chopped

⅓ cup water

⅓ cup vinegar

2 Tbsp. flour

2 Tbsp. sugar

1 tsp. salt

½ tsp. celery seed

¼ tsp. pepper

4 slices bacon, cooked crisp and crumbled

chopped fresh parsley

1. Combine potatoes and onions in slow cooker.

2. Combine remaining ingredients, except bacon and parsley, in bowl. Pour over potatoes.

3. Cover. Cook on Low 8–10 hours, or until potatoes are tender.

4. Stir in bacon and parsley.

5. Serve warm or at room temperature.

Serving Suggestion:
Prepare a full German meal and serve this with grilled bratwurst or sausage, dill pickles, pickled beets, and sliced apples.

Slow-Cooked Baked Beans

Hope Comerford, Clinton Township, MI

Makes 20 or more servings
Prep. Time: 10 minutes   ☙   Soaking Time: 8 hours or overnight
☙   Cooking Time: 12–15 hours   ☙   Ideal slow-cooker size: 7-qt.

2 lb. navy beans, soaked 8 hours or overnight, drained and rinsed

12 oz. salt pork, chopped into small strips

1 large onion, chopped

¾ cup dark brown sugar

1 cup ketchup

3 Tbsp. mustard

7 cups water

1. Place half of the navy beans into the crock with half of the salt pork and half of the onions on top.

2. Mix together the brown sugar, ketchup, and mustard. Pour half of this mixture over the top of the contents of the crock.

3. Add in the remaining navy beans, topped with the remaining salt pork and remaining onions. Pour the rest of the brown sugar mixture over the top.

4. Pour the water into the crock.

5. Cover and cook on Low for 12–15 hours. The longer these cook, the darker the beans will become and the thicker they will get.

"Famous" Baked Beans

Katrine Rose, Woodbridge, VA

Makes 10 servings
Prep. Time: 20 minutes ⚜ Cooking Time: 3–6 hours ⚜ Ideal slow-cooker size: 4-qt.

1 lb. ground beef
¼ cup minced onions
1 cup ketchup
4 15-oz. cans pork and beans
1 cup brown sugar
2 Tbsp. liquid smoke
1 Tbsp. Worcestershire sauce

1. Brown beef and onions in skillet. Stir frequently to break up clumps of meat. Continue cooking until no pink remains in meat. Drain off drippings.

2. Spoon meat and onions into slow cooker.

3. Add remaining ingredients and stir well.

4. Cover. Cook on High 3 hours or on Low 5–6 hours.

NOTE

There are many worthy baked bean recipes, but this is both easy and absolutely delicious. The secret to this recipe is the liquid smoke. I get many requests for this recipe, and some friends have added the word "famous" to its name.

Rudolph's Nose Wild Rice

Darla Sathre, Baxter, MN

Makes 8 servings
Prep. Time: 15 minutes ❧ Cooking Time: 3 hours ❧ Ideal slow-cooker size: 3-qt.

6 cups cooked wild rice, or 3 15-oz. cans wild rice, drained

3.8-oz. can sliced black olives, drained

4-oz. can sliced button mushrooms, rinsed and drained

1 large onion, chopped (about 2 cups)

1 pt. (2 cups) grape, or cherry, tomatoes, halved

8-oz. pkg. cheddar cheese, cubed

¼ cup olive oil

black pepper, to taste

1. Mix all ingredients together gently in slow cooker.

2. Cover. Cook on Low 3 hours.

NOTE

Dear family friends gave us this to use as an oven recipe years ago. We have since adapted it for a slow cooker. While eating it one Christmas Eve, someone commented that the cut tomatoes resembled the reindeer Rudolph's red nose. From then on, we changed the name from Wild Rice Hot Dish to Rudolph's Nose Wild Rice.

TIP

1. The proportions of this recipe can be adjusted to your personal preferences quite easily.

2. When we have just a small amount of leftovers of this recipe, we use it as a pizza topping, and it is delicious!

Holiday Wild Rice

Susan Kasting, Jenks, OK

Makes 4 servings
Prep. Time: 10 minutes   Cooking Time: 2½–3 hours   Ideal slow-cooker size: 4-qt.

1½ cups wild rice, uncooked

3 cups chicken stock

3 Tbsp. orange zest

2 Tbsp. orange juice

½ cup raisins (I like golden raisins)

1½ tsp. curry powder

1 Tbsp. butter, softened

½ cup fresh parsley

½ cup chopped pecans

½ cup chopped green onions

1. Mix rice, chicken stock, orange zest, orange juice, raisins, curry powder, and butter in slow cooker.

2. Cover and cook on High 2½–3 hours, or until rice is tender and has absorbed most of the liquid, but is not dry.

3. Stir in parsley, pecans, and green onion just before serving.

Fruited Wild Rice with Pecans

Dottie Schmidt, Kansas City, MO

Makes 4 servings
Prep. Time: 15 minutes   ♣   Cooking Time: 2–2½ hours   ♣   Ideal slow-cooker size: 3-qt.

½ cup chopped onions

¼ stick (2 Tbsp.) butter, cut in chunks

6-oz. pkg. long-grain and wild rice, uncooked

seasoning packet from wild rice pkg.

1½ cups hot water

⅔ cup apple juice

1 large tart apple, chopped

¼ cup raisins

¼ cup coarsely chopped pecans

1. Combine all ingredients except pecans in greased slow cooker.

2. Cover. Cook on High 2–2½ hours, or until rice is fully cooked.

3. Stir in pecans. Serve.

Broccoli and Rice Casserole

Deborah Swartz, Grottoes, VA

Makes 4–6 servings
Prep. Time: 15–20 minutes   ⚓   Cooking Time: 5–6 hours   ⚓   Ideal slow-cooker size: 3¼-qt.

1 lb. chopped broccoli, fresh or frozen, thawed

1 medium onion, chopped

½ stick (4 Tbsp.) butter, cut in chunks

1 cup instant rice, uncooked, or 1½ cups cooked rice

10¾-oz. can cream of chicken, or mushroom, soup

¼ cup milk

1⅓ cups cubed Velveeta cheese, or shredded cheddar cheese

1 tsp. salt

1. Combine all ingredients in lightly greased slow cooker.

2. Cover. Cook on Low 5–6 hours.

Slow-Cooker Stuffing

Allison Ingels, Maynard, IA

Makes 10–12 servings
Prep. Time: 15 minutes   ❧   Cooking Time: 3 hours   ❧   Ideal slow-cooker size: 5-qt.

12–13 cups dry bread cubes (equal to a 20-oz. loaf of bread)

¼ cup dried parsley

2 eggs, beaten

giblets, cooked and chopped, broth reserved*

1 tsp. salt

¼ tsp. pepper

½ tsp. sage

1½ tsp. poultry seasoning

3½–4½ cups turkey broth (from cooking giblets)

2 chicken bouillon cubes

2 cups finely chopped celery

1 cup finely chopped onions

2 sticks (16 Tbsp.) butter

*Place giblets in 3½–4½ cups water in stockpot. Cover. Cook over medium heat until giblets are tender. Remove giblets from broth and allow them to cool enough to handle. Then cut up giblets and proceed with Step 2. Reserve broth and keep warm in stockpot for Step 3.

1. Combine bread cubes and parsley in slow cooker.

2. Stir in eggs, giblets, and seasonings.

3. Dissolve bouillon in heated turkey broth in stockpot. Add to slow cooker.

4. Sauté celery and onion in butter in stockpot. Stir into bread mixture in slow cooker.

5. Cover. Cook on High 1 hour and then on Low 2 hours, stirring occasionally if you're home and able to do so.

TIP

Making stuffing this way is a convenient way to free up oven space—or keep your kitchen cool.

Variations:

1. Add 1 lb. loose sausage, browned and drained, to Step 2. —Dorothy VanDeest, Memphis, TN

2. Use 6 cups cubed day-old white bread and 6 cups cubed day-old wheat bread to add flavor and fiber. —Jean M. Butzer, Batavia, NY

Slow-Cooker Dressing

Marie Shank, Harrisonburg, VA

Makes 16 servings
Prep. Time: 10 minutes, plus baking time for corn bread ⚜ Cooking Time: 2–8 hours
⚜ Ideal slow-cooker size: 6-qt., or 2 4-qt. cookers

2 boxes Jiffy Corn Muffin Mix
8 slices day-old bread
4 eggs
1 onion, chopped
½ cup chopped celery
2 10¼-oz. cans cream of chicken soup
2 cups chicken broth
1 tsp. salt
½ tsp. pepper
1½ Tbsp. sage, or poultry seasoning
1–1½ sticks (8–12 Tbsp.) butter

1. Prepare corn bread according to package instructions.

2. Crumble corn bread and bread slices together in large bowl.

3. Stir in all other ingredients, except butter.

4. Spoon into 6 qt. greased cooker, or into 2 greased 4-qt. cookers. Dot top(s) with butter.

5. Cover. Cook on High 2–4 hours or on Low 3–8 hours.

Variations:

1. Prepare your favorite corn bread recipe in an 8-inch-square baking pan instead of using corn bread mix.

2. For a more moist dressing, use 2 14½-oz. cans chicken broth instead of 2 cups chicken broth.

3. You may reduce butter to 2 Tbsp. —Helen Kenagy, Carlsbad, NM

Mushroom Stuffing

Laverne Stoner, Scottdale, PA

Makes 7–8 cups stuffing
Prep. Time: 15 minutes   ⚜   Cooking Time: 2–3 hours   ⚜   Ideal slow-cooker size: 5-qt.

1 stick (8 Tbsp.) butter
1 cup finely chopped onions
1 cup finely chopped celery
8-oz. can sliced mushrooms, drained
¼ cup chopped parsley
1½–2 tsp. poultry seasoning
½ tsp. salt
⅛ tsp. pepper
12 cups toasted bread cubes*
2 eggs, well beaten
1½ cups chicken broth

*Lay 18–22 slices of bread on baking sheets. Toast in oven for 15 minutes at 300°F.

TIP

This is not as much a time-saver as it is a space-saver. If your oven is full, make your stuffing in your slow cooker.

1. Sauté onions and celery in butter in skillet until cooked. Stir in mushrooms and parsley.

2. Combine seasonings and sprinkle over bread cubes in large mixing bowl.

3. Gently add remaining ingredients. Spoon lightly into slow cooker.

4. Cover. Cook on High 1 hour, and then reduce to Low and cook 1–2 hours.

Variations:

1. Add extra flavor to your stuffing by adding 1 tsp. dried sage, ¾ tsp. dried thyme, and ¼ tsp. dried marjoram to Step 2.
    —Mary H. Nolt, East Earl, PA
    —Jean Turner, Williams Lake, BC
    —Mary Rogers, Waseca, MN
    —Kristi See, Weskan, KS

2. Add 1 lb. loose sausage, browned and drained, to Step 3. —Dede Peterson, Rapid City, SD

Beverages, Desserts, and Sweets

Hot Chocolate—Peppermint, Dark, and Orange Chocolate

Hope Comerford, Clinton Township, MI

Makes 6 servings

Prep. Time: 5 minutes ⚜ *Cooking Time: 3–4 hours* ⚜ *Ideal slow-cooker size: 3-qt.*

6 cups vitamin D milk, or whatever kind you like

1 tsp. vanilla extract

3½ oz. peppermint bark chocolate, dark chocolate, or orange chocolate

shot of peppermint schnapps or orange schnapps per cup, *optional*

whipped cream, *optional*

1. Place the milk and vanilla into your crock. Cover and cook on Low for 2–3 hours.

2. Break up whichever flavor of chocolate you choose and whisk it into the hot milk.

3. Let it cook an additional hour.

4. Serve each cup with whipped cream on top if you wish. You can also add a shot of peppermint or orange schnapps to each cup before serving for an adult version.

Holiday Cherry Cobbler

Colleen Heatwole, Burton, MI

Makes 5–6 servings
Prep. Time: 15 minutes   ☙   Cooking Time: 2½–3½ hours   ☙   Ideal slow-cooker size: 4-qt.

16-oz. can cherry filling (light or regular)

1 pkg. cake mix for 1 layer white, or yellow, cake

1 egg

3 Tbsp. evaporated milk

½ tsp. cinnamon

½ cup chopped walnuts

1. Spray slow cooker with cooking spray.

2. Spread pie filling in bottom of cooker.

3. Cover. Cook on High 30 minutes.

4. Meanwhile, in a medium-sized mixing bowl mix together cake mix, egg, evaporated milk, cinnamon, and walnuts.

5. Spoon over hot pie filling. Do not stir.

6. Cover. Cook on Low 2–3 hours, or until toothpick inserted in cake layer comes out clean.

Apple Crisp

Michelle Strite, Goshen, IN

Makes 6–8 servings
Prep. Time: 5–10 minutes ⚜ *Cooking Time: 2–3 hours* ⚜ *Ideal slow-cooker size: 2-qt.*

2 21-oz. cans apple pie filling, or:

⅔ cup sugar

1¼ cups water

3 Tbsp. cornstarch

4 cups peeled, sliced apples

½ tsp. ground cinnamon

¼ tsp. ground allspice

¾ cup uncooked quick oatmeal

½ cup brown sugar

½ cup flour

½ stick (4 Tbsp.) butter, at room temperature

1. Place pie filling in slow cooker. If not using prepared filling, combine ⅔ cup sugar, water, cornstarch, apples, cinnamon, and allspice in cooker. Stir until well mixed.

2. In a mixing bowl, combine remaining ingredients until crumbly. Sprinkle over apple filling.

3. Cover. Cook on Low 2–3 hours.

Eggnog Bread Pudding

Hope Comerford, Clinton Township, MI

Makes 6–8 servings
Prep. Time: 15 minutes ♣ Cooking Time: 4–6 hours ♣ Ideal slow-cooker size: 6½-qt.

I cup raisins

½ cup coffee liqueur

8 eggs

2 tsp. vanilla extract

¼ tsp. nutmeg

½ tsp. salt

I cup sugar

4 Tbsp. butter, melted

4 cups eggnog

2 loaves of French bread, cubed and set to dry out over night

whipped cream, *optional*

1. In a small bowl, soak the raisins in the coffee liqueur while you prepare the rest of the ingredients.

2. In a large bowl, whisk together the eggs, vanilla, nutmeg, salt, sugar, melted butter, and eggnog.

3. Pour the raisins and coffee liqueur into the egg mixture and stir.

4. Add the bread cubes to the bowl and stir until every bread cube is well-covered.

5. Spray the crock with nonstick spray, then pour in the coated bread cubes.

6. Cover and cook on Low for 4–6 hours, or until a knife comes out of the center clean.

7. You may wish to place a couple of paper towels under the lid the last hour or two to soak up moisture and thicken the bread pudding.

8. Serve with whipped cream on top if desired.

White Chocolate Bread Pudding

Linda E. Wilcox, Blythewood, SC

Makes 5–6 servings
Prep. Time: 30 minutes ❧ Cooking Time: 1¾ hours ❧ Cooling Time: 30 minutes,
and then 1–2 hours ❧ Ideal slow-cooker size: 3–4-qt.

½ cup dried cranberries, or dried cherries

3 Tbsp. apple cider, or brandy

3-oz. white chocolate bar

6 cups stale French bread, cubed, *divided*

4 eggs

¼ stick (2 Tbsp.) butter, melted

½ cup sugar

1 cup half-and-half

1 tsp. vanilla extract

NOTE
My grandchildren love this dessert.

1. Combine dried fruit with cider or brandy in a microwave-safe bowl.

2. Microwave on High for 30 seconds. Set aside to cool (about 30 minutes).

3. Coarsely chop the white chocolate. Set aside.

4. Drain the dried fruit. Set aside.

5. Spray interior of slow cooker with cooking spray.

6. Cover bottom of slow cooker with half the bread cubes.

7. Sprinkle half the chocolate and half the fruit over bread cubes.

8. Layer in remaining bread cubes. Top with a layer of remaining fruit and a layer of remaining chocolate.

9. In a bowl beat eggs with whisk. Add butter, sugar, half-and-half, and vanilla to eggs. Mix together thoroughly.

10. Pour over bread mixture and press to make sure egg mixture covers all bread.

11. Cover and cook on High 1¾ hours.

12. Cool until warm or at room temperature.

Gingerbread Pudding Cake

Katrina Eberly, Wernersville, PA

Makes 6–8 servings
Prep. Time: 20 minutes ❧ Cooking Time: 2–2½ hours
❧ Standing Time: 15 minutes ❧ Ideal slow-cooker size: 3-qt.

½ stick (4 Tbsp.) butter, softened
¼ cup sugar
1 egg white
1 tsp. vanilla extract
½ cup molasses
1 cup water
1¼ cups flour
¾ tsp. baking soda
½ tsp. ground cinnamon
½ tsp. ground ginger
¼ tsp. salt
¼ tsp. ground allspice
⅛ tsp. ground nutmeg
½ cup chopped pecans
6 Tbsp. brown sugar

Topping:
¾ cup hot water
5⅔ Tbsp. (⅓ cup) butter, melted

1. Spray interior of slow cooker with cooking spray.

2. In a large mixing bowl, cream 4 Tbsp. butter and sugar until light and fluffy. Beat in egg white and vanilla.

3. In a separate bowl, combine molasses and water until blended.

4. In another bowl, combine flour, baking soda, and spices. Add to creamed mixture alternately with molasses mixture, beating well after each addition.

5. Fold in pecans. Spoon into slow cooker. Sprinkle with brown sugar

6. In a small bowl, combine hot water and 5⅔ Tbsp. melted butter. Pour over batter. Do not stir.

7. Cover. Cook on High 2–2½ hours, or until toothpick inserted in center of cake comes out clean.

8. Turn off cooker. Let stand 15 minutes. Serve cake warm.

TIP

from Tester

I used blackstrap molasses, and the flavor didn't overpower the cake.

Pineapple Upside-Down Cake

Vera M. Kuhns, Harrisonburg, VA

Makes 10 servings
Prep. Time: 20 minutes ⚜ Cooking Time: 4–5 hours
⚜ Cooling Time: 10 minutes ⚜ Ideal slow-cooker size: 4-qt.

1 stick (8 Tbsp.) butter, melted

1 cup brown sugar

1 medium-sized can pineapple slices, drained, juice reserved

6–8 maraschino cherries

1 box yellow cake mix

1. Combine butter and brown sugar in well-greased slow cooker. Spread over cooker bottom.

2. Lay pineapple slices over top. Place a cherry in the center of each slice.

3. In a good-sized mixing bowl, prepare cake according to package directions, using pineapple juice for part of liquid.

4. Spoon cake batter into cooker over top fruit.

5. Cover cooker with 2 tea towels and then with its own lid. Cook on High 1 hour, and then on Low 3–4 hours.

6. Insert toothpick in center of cake. If it comes out clean, cake is finished. If it doesn't, continue to cook in 15-minute increments, checking after each one, until pick comes out clean.

7. Allow cake to cool for 10 minutes. Then run knife around edge and invert cake onto large platter.

Orange Slice Cake

Steven Lantz, Denver, CO

Makes 10–12 servings
Prep. Time: 20 minutes   ♣   Cooking Time: 2–3 hours
♣   Cooling Time: 3–4 hours   ♣   Ideal slow-cooker size: 3-qt.

I cup chopped dates

½ lb. candied orange slices, cut into thirds

½ cup chopped walnuts

I cup flaked, unsweetened coconut

I Tbsp. grated orange rind, *optional*

1¾ cups flour, *divided*

I stick (8 Tbsp.) butter, at room temperature

I cup sugar

2 eggs

½ tsp. baking soda

¼ cup buttermilk

1. In a good-sized mixing bowl, combine dates, orange slices, walnuts, coconut, and orange rind if you wish.

2. Pour ¼ cup flour over mixture and stir together.

3. In a separate big bowl, cream butter and sugar together. Add eggs and beat well.

4. In a small bowl, dissolve baking soda in buttermilk.

5. Add remaining 1½ cups flour and buttermilk, in which soda has been dissolved, to creamed mixture.

6. Stir in fruit and nut mixture.

7. Pour into greased slow cooker.

8. Cover. Cook on High 2–3 hours, or until toothpick inserted in center comes out clean.

9. Allow cake to cool completely before removing from slow cooker.

TIP

from Tester

I chopped the dates and nuts in my food processor. I spooned them into a mixing bowl where I combined them with the other ingredients in Steps 1 and 2. Then I continued using my food processor for Steps 3 and 5. No need to wash it in between. I believe in saving time whenever I can.

NOTE

This cake is perfect with coffee in the morning or later in the day as dessert.

Carrot Cake

Colleen Heatwole, Burton, MI

Makes 6–8 servings

Prep. Time: 20 minutes ❧ Cooking Time: 3–4 hours ❧ Ideal slow-cooker size: large enough to hold your baking insert

½ cup vegetable oil

2 eggs

1 Tbsp. hot water

½ cup grated raw carrots

¾ cup flour

¾ cup sugar

½ tsp. baking powder

⅛ tsp. salt

¼ tsp. ground allspice

½ tsp. ground cinnamon

⅛ tsp. ground cloves

½ cup chopped nuts

½ cup raisins, or chopped dates

2 Tbsp. flour

1. In large bowl, beat oil, eggs, and water for 1 minute.

2. Add carrots. Mix well.

3. In a separate bowl, stir together flour, sugar, baking powder, salt, allspice, cinnamon, and cloves. Add to creamed mixture.

4. Toss nuts and raisins in bowl with 2 Tbsp. flour. Add to creamed mixture. Mix well.

5. Pour into greased and floured 3-lb. shortening can or slow-cooker baking insert. Place can or baking insert in slow cooker.

6. Cover insert with its lid, or cover can with 8 paper towels, folded down over edge of slow cooker to absorb moisture. Cover paper towels with cooker lid. Cook on High 3–4 hours, or until toothpick inserted in center of cake comes out clean.

7. Remove can or insert from cooker and allow to cool on rack for 10 minutes. Run knife around edge of cake. Invert onto serving plate.

Easy Easy Cake

Janice Muller, Derwood, MD

Makes 8–10 servings
Prep. Time: 10 minutes ⚘ Cooking Time: 2–3 hours ⚘ Ideal slow-cooker size: 3½-qt.

20-oz. can crushed pineapple, undrained

21-oz. can blueberry, or cherry, pie filling

18½-oz. pkg. yellow cake mix

cinnamon

1 stick (8 Tbsp.) butter, cut into chunks

1 cup chopped nuts

vanilla ice cream or whipped cream

1. Grease bottom and sides of interior of slow cooker.

2. Spread a layer of pineapple in bottom.

3. Top with a layer of pie filling.

4. Top that with a layer of dry cake mix. Be careful not to mix the layers!

5. Sprinkle with cinnamon.

6. Top with thin layers of butter chunks and nuts.

7. Cover cooker. Cook on High 2–3 hours, or until toothpick inserted in center comes out clean.

8. Serve warm with vanilla ice cream or whipped cream.

Variation:

Substitute a pkg. of spice cake mix and apple pie filling.

Creamy Orange Cheesecake

Jeanette Oberholtzer, Manheim, PA

Makes 10 servings

Prep. Time: 15 minutes ❧ Cooking Time: 2½–3 hours ❧ Standing Time: 1–2 hours
❧ Chilling Time: 2–4 hours ❧ Ideal slow-cooker size: large enough to hold your baking insert

Crust:

¾ cup graham cracker crumbs

2 Tbsp. sugar

3 Tbsp. melted butter

Filling:

2 8-oz. pkgs. cream cheese, at room temperature

⅔ cup sugar

2 eggs

1 egg yolk

¼ cup frozen orange juice concentrate

1 tsp. orange zest

1 Tbsp. flour

½ tsp. vanilla extract

1. Combine crust ingredients in a small bowl. Pat into 7- or 9-inch springform pan, whichever size fits into your slow cooker.

2. In a large mixing bowl, cream together cream cheese and sugar. Add eggs and yolk. Beat 3 minutes.

3. Add juice, zest, flour, and vanilla. Beat 2 more minutes.

4. Pour batter into crust. Place on rack (or jar rings) in slow cooker.

5. Cover. Cook on High 2½–3 hours. Turn off and let stand 1–2 hours, or until cool enough to remove from cooker.

6. Cool completely before removing sides of pan. Chill before serving.

Serving suggestion:

Serve with thawed frozen whipped topping and fresh or mandarin orange slices.

Slow-Cooker Pumpkin Pie

Colleen Heatwole, Burton, MI

Makes 5–6 servings
Prep. Time: 10 minutes ♣ Cooking Time: 3–4 hours
♣ Cooling Time: 2–4 hours ♣ Ideal slow-cooker size: 3-qt.

15-oz. can solid-pack pumpkin

12-oz. can evaporated milk

¾ cup sugar

½ cup low-fat buttermilk baking mix

2 eggs, beaten

¼ stick (2 Tbsp.) butter, melted

1 ½ tsp. cinnamon

¾ tsp. ground ginger

¼ tsp. ground nutmeg

whipped topping

1. Spray slow cooker with cooking spray.

2. Mix all ingredients together in slow cooker, except whipped topping.

3. Cover. Cook on Low 3–4 hours, or until a toothpick inserted in center comes out clean.

4. Allow to cool to warm, or chill, before serving with whipped topping.

Variation:

You can substitute 2. Tbsp. pumpkin pie spice in place of cinnamon, ginger, and nutmeg.

Christmas Apple Date Pudding

Colleen Heatwole, Burton, MI

Makes 8 servings
Prep. Time: 30 minutes ❧ Cooking Time: 3–4 hours ❧ Ideal slow-cooker size: 2-qt.

4–5 apples, peeled, cored, and diced
½ cup sugar
½ cup chopped dates
½ cup toasted, chopped pecans
1 Tbsp. flour
1 tsp. baking powder
⅛ tsp. salt
½ tsp. cinnamon
2 Tbsp. melted butter
1 beaten egg

1. In a greased slow cooker, mix together apples, sugar, dates, and pecans.

2. In a separate bowl, mix together flour, baking powder, salt, and cinnamon. Stir into apple mixture.

3. Drizzle melted butter over batter and stir.

4. Stir in egg.

5. Cover. Cook on Low 3–4 hours. Serve warm.

Steamed Chocolate Pudding

Evelyn L. Ward, Greeley, CO

Makes 8 servings

Prep. Time: 10 minutes ☙ Cooking Time: 2½ hours ☙ Ideal slow-cooker size: large enough to hold your baking insert or a coffee can standing upright

1 stick (8 Tbsp.) butter, softened
¾ cup sugar
¾ cup flour
3 Tbsp. cocoa powder
¼ tsp. salt
3 eggs
½ tsp. vanilla extract
¼ cup half-and-half

1. Cream together butter and sugar with electric mixer.

2. In a separate bowl, sift together flour, cocoa powder, and salt.

3. Add flour mixture alternately with eggs to creamed mixture. Beat well.

4. Add vanilla and half-and-half. Beat well.

5. Spoon into greased and floured slow cooker baking insert. Cover tightly with lid or double layer of foil.

6. Place insert on a rack in slow cooker. Add boiling water to slow cooker, halfway up sides of insert.

7. Cover slow cooker. Cook on High 2½ hours.

8. Remove insert from cooker. Cool 2 minutes. Unmold.

TIP

1. A coffee can that stands upright inside your slow cooker serves as a good pudding mold.

2. You can use a jar ring for a rack under the can or baking insert.

Serving Suggestion:
Cut into wedges. Serve with frozen whipped topping, thawed, or ice cream.

Beverages, Desserts, and Sweets ❧ 307

Slow-Cooker Rice Pudding

Dede Peterson, Rapid City, SD

Makes 5 servings

Prep. Time: 10 minutes ♣ Cooking Time: 3–4 hours ♣ Cooling Time: 2–5 hours ♣ Ideal slow-cooker size: 2-qt.

1 pkg. vanilla cook-and-serve pudding mix

1 cup cooked white rice

1 cup raisins

1 tsp. cinnamon

2 tsp. vanilla extract

3 cups half-and-half, or milk

1. Combine all ingredients in slow cooker.

2. Cover. Cook on Low 3–4 hours.

3. Serve warm, at room temperature, or chilled.

Eggnog Gingersnap Custard

Sue Hamilton, Minooka, IL

Makes 4–6 servings
Prep. Time: 5 minutes ❧ Cooking Time: 3½–4 hours
❧ Cooling/Chilling Time: 20 minutes–4 hours ❧ Ideal slow-cooker size: 3–4-qt.

24 small gingersnaps
4 eggs
1 qt. eggnog

1. Spray interior of slow cooker with cooking spray.

2. Lay all cookies on bottom of slow cooker.

3. In a large mixing bowl, beat eggs. Stir in eggnog.

4. Slowly pour mixture into slow cooker. The cookies will rise in a layer to the top.

5. Cover. Cook on Low 3½–4 hours, or until custard is set.

6. Remove cover. Let cool 20 minutes for a warm custard, or chill 4 or more hours for a cold custard.

Cranberry Baked Apples

Judi Manos, West Islip, NY

Makes 4 servings

Prep. Time: 15 minutes ⚜ Cooking Time: 4–6 hours ⚜ Ideal slow-cooker size: 4–5-qt.

⅓ cup packed brown sugar

¼ cup dried cranberries

4 large cooking apples

½ cup cranberry-apple juice cocktail

¼ stick (2 Tbsp.) butter, melted

½ tsp. ground cinnamon

¼ tsp. ground nutmeg

chopped nuts, *optional*

1. In a small bowl, mix brown sugar and cranberries together.

2. Core apples but leave whole. Fill centers with brown sugar and cranberry mixture.

3. Set apples upright in slow cooker. (Don't stack them.)

4. In the same small bowl, combine cranberry-apple juice and melted butter. Pour over apples.

5. Sprinkle with cinnamon and nutmeg.

6. Cover. Cook on Low 4–6 hours.

7. To serve, spoon sauce over apples and sprinkle with nuts.

Serving Suggestion:
A great accompaniment to vanilla ice cream.

NOTE

This was one of our favorite recipes while growing up. When it's cooking, the house smells delicious. I'm suddenly full of memories of days gone by and a much more relaxing time. My mother passed away in October, and I found this recipe among her collection of favorites.

Graham Cracker Cookies

Cassandra Ly, Carlisle, PA

Makes 8 dozen cookies

Prep. Time: 10 minutes & Cooking Time: 1½ hours & Ideal slow-cooker size: 4-qt.

12-oz. pkg. (2 cups) semisweet chocolate chips

2 1-oz. squares unsweetened baking chocolate, shaved

2 14-oz. cans sweetened condensed milk

3¾ cups crushed graham cracker crumbs, *divided*

1 cup finely chopped walnuts

1. Place chocolate chips and shaved chocolate in slow cooker.

2. Cover. Cook on High 1 hour, stirring every 15 minutes. Continue to cook on Low, stirring every 15 minutes, or until chocolate is melted (about 30 minutes more).

3. Stir milk into melted chocolate.

4. Add 3 cups graham cracker crumbs, 1 cup at a time, stirring after each addition.

5. Stir in nuts. Mixture should be thick but not stiff.

6. Stir in remaining graham cracker crumbs until batter is consistency of cookie dough.

7. Drop by heaping teaspoonfuls onto lightly greased cookie sheets. Keep remaining mixture warm by covering and turning slow cooker to Warm.

8. Bake at 325°F for 7–9 minutes, or until tops of cookies begin to crack. Remove from oven. Cool 1–2 minutes on rack before transferring to waxed paper.

NOTE

This delectable fudge-like cookie is a family favorite. The original recipe (from my maternal grandmother) was so involved and yielded so few cookies that my mom and I would get together to make a couple of batches only at Christmastime. Adapting the recipe for a slow cooker, rather than a double boiler, allows me to prepare a double batch without help.

TIP

These cookies freeze well.

Chocolate-Covered Pretzels

Beth Maurer, Harrisonburg, VA

Makes 10–12 servings

Prep. Time: 10 minutes ❧ Cooking Time: 30–60 minutes ❧ Ideal slow-cooker size: 2-qt.

1 lb. white chocolate bark coating

2 blocks chocolate bark coating

1 bag pretzel rods

1. Chop white chocolate into small chunks. Place in slow cooker.

2. Cover. Heat on Low setting, stirring occasionally until melted, about 30 minutes. Turn off cooker.

3. Using a spoon, coat ¾ of each pretzel rod with chocolate. Place on waxed paper to cool.

4. Chop chocolate bark into small chunks. Microwave on High in a microwave-safe bowl for 1½ minutes. Stir. Microwave on High 1 more minute. Stir.

5. Microwave on High in 30-second intervals until chocolate is smooth when stirred. (Do not allow chocolate to get too hot or it will scorch.)

6. Put melted chocolate in small bag. Snip off corner of bag. Drizzle chocolate over white chocolate-covered pretzels.

TIP

These are easy to make. They also taste wonderful and are good holiday gifts when thoroughly cooled and placed in small gift bags!

Chocolate Fondue

Vera Schmucker, Goshen, IN
Vicki Dinkel, Sharon Springs, KS

Makes 8–10 servings
Prep. Time: 10 minutes ⚶ Cooking Time: 3–7 hours ⚶ Ideal slow-cooker size: 3½-qt.

1 Tbsp. butter

16 1-oz. chocolate candy bars with almonds, unwrapped and broken

30 large marshmallows

1⅓ cups milk, *divided*

angel food cake cubes; strawberries; chunks of pineapple, bananas, apples, or oranges; pretzel pieces

1. Grease slow cooker with butter. Turn to High for 10 minutes.

2. Add chocolate, marshmallows, and ⅓ cup milk.

3. Cover. Turn cooker to Low. Stir after 30 minutes.

4. Continue cooking for another 30 minutes, or until mixture is melted and smooth.

5. Gradually add remaining milk.

5. Cover. Cook on Low 2–6 hours.

6. Bring cooker to table, along with angel food cake, fruit, and pretzels for dipping.

Equivalent Measurements

dash = little less than $\frac{1}{8}$ tsp.

3 tsp. = 1 Tbsp.

2 Tbsp. = 1 oz.

4 Tbsp. = ¼ cup

5 Tbsp. plus 1 tsp. = $\frac{1}{3}$ cup

8 Tbsp. = ½ cup

12 Tbsp. = ¾ cup

16 Tbsp. = 1 cup

1 cup = 8 oz. liquid

2 cups = 1 pt.

4 cups = 1 qt.

4 qt. = 1 gal.

1 stick butter = ¼ lb.

1 stick butter = ½ cup

1 stick butter = 8 Tbsp.

beans, 1 lb. dried = 2–2½ cups (depending on the size of the beans)

bell pepper, 1 large = 1 cup chopped

cheese, hard (for example, cheddar, Swiss, Monterey Jack, mozzarella), 1 lb. grated = 4 cups

cheese, cottage, 1 lb. = 2 cups

chocolate chips, 6-oz. pkg. = 1 scant cup

crackers (butter, saltines, snack), 20 single crackers = 1 cup crumbs

herbs, 1 Tbsp. fresh = 1 tsp. dried

lemon, 1 medium-sized = 2–3 Tbsp. juice

lemon, 1 medium-sized = 2–3 tsp. grated rind

mustard, 1 Tbsp. prepared = 1 tsp. dry or ground mustard

oatmeal, 1 lb. dry = about 5 cups dry

onion, 1 medium-sized = ½ cup chopped

Pasta

macaroni, penne, and other small or tubular shapes, 1 lb. dry = 4 cups uncooked

noodles, 1 lb. dry = 6 cups uncooked

spaghetti, linguine, fettucine, 1 lb. dry = 4 cups uncooked

potatoes, white, 1 lb. = 3 medium-sized potatoes = 2 cups mashed

Potatoes, sweet, 1 lb. = 3 medium-sized potatoes = 2 cups mashed

rice, 1 lb. dry = 2 cups uncooked

sugar, confectioners', 1 lb. = 3½ cups sifted

whipping cream, 1 cup unwhipped = 2 cups whipped

whipped topping, 8-oz. container = 3 cups

yeast, dry, 1 envelope (¼ oz.) = 1 Tbsp.

Assumptions about Ingredients

flour = unbleached or white, and all-purpose

oatmeal or oats = dry, quick or rolled (old-fashioned), unless specified

pepper = black, finely ground

rice = regular, long-grain (not instant unless specified)

salt = table salt

shortening = solid, not liquid

sugar = granulated sugar (not brown and not confectioners')

Substitute Ingredients

For 1 cup buttermilk—use 1 cup plain yogurt; or pour 1^1/$_3$ Tbsp. lemon juice or vinegar into a 1-cup measure. Fill the cup with milk. Stir and let stand for 5 minutes. Stir again before using.

For 1 oz. unsweetened baking chocolate—stir together 3 Tbsp. unsweetened cocoa powder and 1 Tbsp. butter, softened.

For 1 Tbsp. cornstarch—use 2 Tbsp. all-purpose flour; or 4 tsp. instant tapioca.

For 1 garlic clove—use ¼ tsp. garlic salt (reduce salt in recipe by ⅛ tsp.); or ⅛ tsp. garlic powder.

For 1 Tbsp. fresh herbs—use 1 tsp. dried herbs.

For 8 oz. fresh mushrooms—use 1 4-oz. can mushrooms, drained.

For 1 Tbsp. prepared mustard—use 1 tsp. dry or ground mustard.

For 1 medium-sized fresh onion—use 2 Tbsp. minced dried onion; or 2 tsp. onion salt (reduce salt in recipe by 1 tsp.); or 1 tsp. onion powder. Note: These substitutions will work for meatballs and meatloaf, but not for sautéing.

For 1 cup sour milk—use 1 cup plain yogurt; or pour 1 Tbsp. lemon juice or vinegar into a 1-cup measure. Fill with milk. Stir and then let stand for 5 minutes. Stir again before using.

For 2 Tbsp. tapioca—use 3 Tbsp. all-purpose flour.

For 1 cup canned tomatoes—use 1^1/$_3$ cups diced fresh tomatoes, cooked gently for 10 minutes.

For 1 Tbsp. tomato paste—use 1 Tbsp. ketchup.

For 1 Tbsp. vinegar—use 1 Tbsp. lemon juice.

For 1 cup heavy cream—add ¾ cup melted butter to ¾ cup milk. Note: This will work for baking and cooking, but not for whipping.

For 1 cup whipping cream—chill thoroughly ⅔ cup evaporated milk, plus the bowl and beaters, then whip; or use 2 cups store-bought whipped topping.

For ½ cup wine—pour 2 Tbsp. wine vinegar into a ½-cup measure. Fill with broth (chicken, beef, or vegetable). Stir and then let stand for 5 minutes. Stir again before using.

Index

About the Author

Hope Comerford is a mom, wife, elementary music teacher, blogger, recipe developer, public speaker, Young Living Essential Oils essential oil enthusiast/educator, and published author. In 2013, she was diagnosed with a severe gluten intolerance and since then has spent many hours creating easy, practical, and delicious gluten-free recipes that can be enjoyed by both those who are affected by gluten and those who are not.

Growing up, Hope spent many hours in the kitchen with her Meme (grandmother) and her love for cooking grew from there. While working on her master's degree when her daughter was young, Hope turned to her slow cookers for some salvation and sanity. It was from there she began truly experimenting with recipes and quickly learned she had the ability to get a little more creative in the kitchen and develop her own recipes.

In 2010, Hope started her blog, *A Busy Mom's Slow Cooker Adventures*, to simply share the recipes she was making with her family and friends. She never imagined people all over the world would begin visiting her page and sharing her recipes with others as well. In 2013, Hope self-published her first cookbook, *Slow Cooker Recipes: 10 Ingredients or Less and Gluten-Free*, and then later wrote *The Gluten-Free Slow Cooker*.

Hope became the new brand ambassador and author of Fix-It and Forget-It in mid-2016. She is excited to bring her creativeness to the Fix-It and Forget-It brand. Through Fix-It and Forget-It, she has written *Fix-It and Forget-It Lazy and Slow*; *Fix-It and Forget-It Healthy Slow Cooker Cookbook*; *Fix-It and Forget-It Favorite Slow Cooker Recipes for Mom*; *Fix-It and Forget-It Favorite Slow Cooker Recipes for Dad*; and *Welcome Home Cookbook*.

Hope lives in the city of Clinton Township, Michigan, near Metro Detroit. She's lived in Michigan her whole life. She has been happily married to her husband and best friend, Justin, since 2008. Together they have two children, Ella and Gavin, who are her motivation, inspiration, and heart. In her spare time, Hope enjoys traveling, singing, cooking, reading books, spending time with friends and family, and relaxing.